Big Hand, Little Hand

A Mum's Story of Love, Hope and Loss

TRISH CARPENTER

First published by Ultimate World Publishing 2019
Copyright © 2019 Trish Carpenter

ISBN

Paperback - 978-1-925884-85-2
Ebook - 978-1-925884-86-9

Trish Carpenter has asserted her right under the Copyright, Designs and Patents Act 1988 to be identified as the author of this work. The information in this book is based on the author's experiences and opinions. The publisher specifically disclaims responsibility for any adverse consequences, which may result from use of the information contained herein. Permission to use information has been sought by the author. Any breaches will be rectified in further editions of the book.

All rights reserved. No part of this publication may be reproduced, stored in or introduced into a retrieval system, or transmitted in any form, or by any means (electronic, mechanical, photocopying, recording or otherwise) without the prior written permission of the author. Any person who does any unauthorised act in relation to this publication may be liable to criminal prosecution and civil claims for damages. Enquiries should be made through the publisher.

Cover design: Ultimate World Publishing
Layout and typesetting: Ultimate World Publishing
Editor: James Salmon

Ultimate World Publishing
Diamond Creek,
Victoria Australia 3089
www.writeabook.com.au

Testimonials

No parent should ever have to bury their own child. No child should have to bury their twin brother. Tom's courageous fight against brain cancer is devastatingly recounted by his mother, Trish Carpenter in her memoir *Big Hand, Little Hand*. It is a story of one child's strength and his mother's unwavering love. It is also a way to cope with unimaginable grief and may provide some solace for those who are forced to face similar adversity in their lives. Unique in its subject matter and perspective, this book is a must-read for parents or loved ones of children who have been touched by cancer.

Helen O'Rourke: teacher and parent

Filled with practical advice, *Big Hand, Little Hand* is essential reading for parents, co-parents and supporters of any child and family who experiences brain cancer. Trish has beautifully captured her son Tom's cheeky spirit and courage in the face of an unbearable fight. The help this book will give other parents and families is a tribute to Tom, and just one example of how his legacy lives on. Vale Tom the Superhero, and thank you Trish for selflessly sharing your experiences to help others.

Trudi Plaschke: writer and editor

Big Hand, Little Hand is a beautiful, raw and honest sharing of a family's incredible fight when Thomas, their beautiful, active, and creative boy is diagnosed with cancer and a brain injury. This book is Tom's story; of his cheeky personality, his beautiful and amazing adventures, and his heroic bravery. It is also his mum's story, a story of endless love and commitment, of tears and laughter, of music and memories as she negotiates this new and foreign world. In being able to share both intimate details of her grief, as well as practical advice around the everyday challenges faced when your child is diagnosed with a serious illness and injury, Trish has created a much-needed resource for other parents who may be in a similar position. As professionals, we can offer guidance, counselling and advice for families faced with enormous struggles such as this, but to hear from the perspective of another parent is immensely valuable in validating others' experiences and supporting others navigating their own difficult path. This book is both a powerful tribute to Tom, and an amazing gift to try and help others.

Alana English: Senior Social Worker
QLD Paediatric Rehabilitation Service

Big Hand, Little Hand chronicles two courageous thirteen-month struggles. The first is Thomas', a seven-year-old twin diagnosed with a brain tumour, who faces every attendant treatment to rid him of disease with a stoicism beyond his years. The second struggle is that of his mother, thrown into a world she has little knowledge of, wants no part of and has no arsenal for facing the impact of her son's diagnosis.

Part memoir, part guide for others experiencing similar issues, and wholly an honest and confronting account, *Big Hand, Little Hand* captures the heartbreak and pain of accompanying and mothering a young child on a horrendous journey. It is a journey not undertaken alone and yet against the background of medical intervention and hospital care the strength of the relationship between Tom and his mother is what resonates strongly throughout.

Theirs is a story told with great poignancy. A difficult and sometimes unsettling read, *Big Hand, Little Hand* is nonetheless a gift – a tribute to a beautiful boy and a celebration of the love that surrounded and sustained him.

**Jane Connolly:
former nurse, teacher, teacher librarian, bookseller, reviewer, literary awards judge and corporate communicator.**

Note from the Author

It should be noted that all details relating to research, statistics and treatment protocols listed in the book and more specifically in the appendices are accurate at time of writing and publication (2019).

Reference to the Lady Cilento Children's Hospital (LCCH): During our time of diagnosis and treatment, this was the name of the hospital we attended. In the following year, the name of this hospital was changed to Queensland Children's Hospital.

This book is written from an Australian perspective, and therefore the health care details, treatment, charities and organisations may be specific to this country.

A portion of the profits from the sale of this book will be donated to charities dedicated to tackling childhood cancer.

For my darling Thomas. May this book be a record of your humble bravery, your sweet nature and your unbreakable spirit. You inspire me every day. You will always be remembered – I promise. You are my star, my son – I'm the luckiest mum in the world.

Love you Bubba.

Contents

Testimonials iii
Note from the Author vii
Dedication ix
Introduction xiii
Chapter 1: A Fear of Small Rooms 1
Chapter 2: Back to Square One 17
Chapter 3: A New Home 29
Chapter 4: Ringing the Bells 47
Chapter 5: High Hopes 63
Chapter 6: Another Small Room 81
Chapter 7: Bucket List Days 97
Chapter 8: The 'Pal' I Never Wanted 115
Chapter 9: The Importance of a Hummingbird 125
Chapter 10: A Superhero Takes Flight 135
Chapter 11: No Such Thing 151
Chapter 12: A Table for Two 165
Acknowledgments 185
Appendix 1: Brain Cancer 189
Appendix 2: Brain Injury 205
Appendix 3: Palliative Care 211
Appendix 4: Other Support Services and Charities 215
Reference List 221
About the Author 231

Introduction

Motivation and premise of the book

Whenever I am confronted with something new, I go looking for ways to understand it, to prepare myself, to learn, so I have the best chance of being able to handle it. Why guess my way along, when others have been through what I was about to face? When I struggled to fall pregnant, I began my investigations into IVF. When I fell pregnant with two, I devoured books on handling and rearing identical twins. When I found out I was having boys, as a woman with three sisters and no real experience with little boys, I searched for books with advice on dealing with the important issues surrounding the raising of boys.

When cancer and brain injury impacted my family – my beautiful six-year-old son – it was so devastating and foreign to me. I went to my 'go-to' on new challenges and started looking for information. There are pamphlets out there, children's books, medical journals and research. There are a lot of books about cancer as experienced by adults. I couldn't find many books that were written for parents with children who suffer from cancer. Even less about the brain injury of posterior fossa syndrome. Although there are many reasons why writing this book is important to me, the motivation for this book comes from a hope to help other parents who find themselves in my position. I think a book like this would have helped me, knowing that other parents have lived through their child's diagnosis and have found ways to empower these brave little souls. Know that you are not alone in dealing with the difficulties around care, parenting and the horror of serious illness and injury when it happens to your child. Perhaps hearing it from another parent is another way of understanding, another more relatable perspective that might help. And trust me, there will be long waits in the hospital so having a book to read is always a good way to pass the time.

Thomas and Me

My boys were born in January of 2011 after a year of IVF treatments, identical twin boys named Cameron and Thomas. These baby boys were my everything, the way each new baby is to each new parent. I loved watching them grow and learn together and then to start to differentiate from each other. Thomas was quick on developing his physical skills while Cameron was first on verbal communication. I could talk on and on about both of my sons but for the purposes of this book, Thomas is the focus. This is my journey with Tom as he battled brain cancer.

If I were asked to describe Thomas in the years before his diagnosis, I would say he was cheeky, active, bright, kind, competitive and creative. He loved to dance, to visit the beach, play in the waves and to run. Tom was tall and skinny and had a scar on his lip from a quick-moving piece of playground equipment. He could take a hit better than most though and loved to wrestle with his brother Cam. Thomas showed imagination and spontaneity every day and

INTRODUCTION

he had a keen sense of justice. He loved symmetry, puzzling things out and he had a very curious mind.

When asked about the boy Thomas became after his diagnosis in December of 2017, I would say he was still all of these things, but I saw such an amazing level of courage, of resilience, of perseverance and strength develop in my lanky boy. When adults are faced with hardship in their life, we would hope these qualities would be somewhere inside to help us cope with the worst time of our lives. I never expected to see a child handle this terrible situation with such grace, humour and courage. But that's what I saw. What a lucky mum I am to have such a wonderful child, who matured beyond his years in so many ways.

As for me, I grew up in a happy, middle class family in Brisbane, Australia. I am a high school teacher of music and history. Music is particularly important to me. It's always in my head, it's attached to memories. I use it as a tool to better understand the world and my life. It's been a mechanism through which I've found comfort and inspiration when confronted with emotional distress and trauma. Each chapter I reference a piece of music. The poetry of these beautiful songs helped me then and continue to, even now. I recommend listening to these songs (in bold) as you read through. The track list for the book is listed in the reference notes and the link to the Spotify Playlist – *Big Hand, Little Hand* is http://bit.ly/bighandlittlehand-soundtrack.

Tom's father and I are divorced, and we had both re-partnered before this story began in December 2017. He and I shared the care of Thomas during his treatments over thirteen months. This happened in a fairly pragmatic and scheduled way, swapping shifts at the hospital, writing updates for each other in a little book, etc.

I did not have a close-up view or understanding of cancer prior to the discovery of Tom's tumour, apart from what you see in the movies. Things like … people with cancer lose their hair. They feel sick and weak all of the time. Some survive it and some do not. I had some experience with brain injury and rehabilitation as my father had suffered strokes over the previous ten years before he passed away in 2017. My only medical background or skill before all of this was administering IVF medications to myself. Apart from that, I kept a bottle of Panadol in the cupboard next to the Vicks, antiseptic and band aids. The basics of a parent's first aid kit really. I was as unprepared as most parents are when suddenly faced with childhood cancer.

The Broader Experience

I am very aware that my experience is not the only one out there. Every child's diagnosis comes with its own complications and treatments. I know that families have different dynamics and relationships. This book does not suggest that the way my story went will be the way any other would play out. The way I coped is not the only way to cope. I went back to speak with the health practitioners at Tom's hospital to get a broader understanding of how they witness parents deal with the world of childhood cancer and rehabilitation. I also wanted to know more about their experiences of how they see children cope.

If parts of this book have similarities to others' experiences, then I hope they would pick and choose what is helpful. Find comfort in our anecdotes. I have included a summary of practical advice at the end of each chapter which sits separate from the narrative. My hope is that these dot points might be helpful for those going through some of this or for supporters of parents that are. Be free to take or leave my advice. Whether you are a parent dealing with some of these challenges, or even if you're not, I hope you can find resonance in Tom's story and my journey as his mum.

This book is our story, of Thomas and me. It chronicles the happenings of Tom's battle with brain cancer and brain injury. The

INTRODUCTION

story of our entwined experiences through all that we endured and how we coped; the wins, the losses and everything in between. It is a clear recollection of how he became a hero to me as he fought each battle in every hospital room, operating theatre and therapy session. This book is in the name of Tom's memory and his legacy of courage.

We remember him in our conversations, our celebrations and our quiet moments of reflection

Chapter 1

A Fear of Small Rooms

Medulloblastoma

Tom was always tired. At least in the months leading up to our arrival at the emergency room. I had been planning on taking my family on a cruise and we were days away from departure. He'd had random incidences of vomiting, sometimes headaches and a slight loss of appetite but the most intense difference for Tom was his exhaustion. Blood tests came back normal and the GP suggested perhaps…just a virus? One weekend after his swimming lesson, Tom had issues with his sight, balance and speech. After a long daytime nap and a weary afternoon, he was back to normal and ready for school on Monday. With new symptoms now, the GP suggested an MRI, but no information came through during the week about an appointment. In the final week of school, Thomas wasn't making it through the school day. After a paediatrician appointment on the Friday, it was recommended that Thomas stay home instead of embarking on the family cruise. Still no word on the MRI at this point and I was hoping on that last day of school when I picked Thomas up there would be something. Something to necessitate a visit to the emergency room for some clear answers. He came home feeling fine and looking forward to the start of the summer holidays. So we stayed home.

The next day, the 9th December, I took the boys for their Saturday morning swimming lesson, as we always did. I'm not sure why I recall that morning with such clarity. I watched the boys in their lesson as they listened only half the time but had a ball. Cam got out to visit the bathroom and I watched him run alongside the pool. Soon after, Thomas followed and for some unknown reason, raced all the way to the outside bathrooms past the lap pool. I can still see him in his yellow swimming shorts and rashie, running with straight arms and goggles on his face, dashing out the doors. It was the last time I saw him run.

While the boys had a play in the pool after their lesson I made an appointment with the GP for later that morning. Tom got out after a while and wanted to sit with me while we waited for Cam to finish up playing. We talked about chocolate, I videoed him talking in a funny voice which he put on all for the sake of the camera and he made me laugh. Thomas walked with me back to the car while Cam ran ahead. It was hot that day and I was overheated. Thomas would often offer to cool me down with his cold, wrinkly swimming hands by pressing them against my cheeks. I dropped Cameron at my mum's and took Thomas off to the doctor, ready to fight for an MRI so we could finally get an idea if there was anything serious going on.

By the time we arrived at the GP, Tom was failing. His thumb was in his mouth and he was falling asleep at only 11:30am. We went in to wait and after a few minutes, Tom's head was in his hands and he couldn't open his eyes. His headache and exhaustion was so great. He wanted to sit on my lap for a cuddle so he could sleep. Finally, we were called into the room and Tom woke for a bit. After a quick examination, the doctor suggested we head straight to the Emergency Room at Lady Cilento Children's Hospital and wrote me a letter to hasten our admission process and to request an MRI to be scheduled urgently. Tom complained of feeling sick and vomited all over the floor.

Becoming more anxious by the minute, I drove to the hospital. I'd called my partner, Owen, and asked him to meet us if he could get away from work. By the time we arrived, Tom couldn't walk straight or with any speed. His balance was gone but he didn't realise it and I had to carry him from the carpark to the nurse's desk. My gangly six-year-old boy was heavier than I realised but we made it. Tom was quickly assigned a bed for examinations and observations to start. After telling the doctors how he had deteriorated that morning there was no more wait for an MRI and arrangements were made quickly. Tom was so patient and affable with the nurses even when they took his blood. We returned from 'Imaging' in the late afternoon and Owen had joined the nurses who were having a play with Thomas, thoroughly charmed by his cheeky chatter. Some policemen who were visiting the ward came to say hello. Loving the attention and with a big smile on his dial now that some of his tiredness had passed, he didn't notice when the doctor asked me to follow her.

As worried as I was, I didn't think there was something overly serious going on with Tom. Nothing that couldn't be fixed with medication or perhaps a diet change or something innocuous like that. I didn't even notice that I was being led to a small room. That should have been my first clue. I had been in a small room with a doctor before. Ten years prior, doctors told my mum and I that my father was not going to recover from his stroke. That, unless he developed a cough, he would develop pneumonia and be gone by the end of the week. Fortunately, my Dad did develop a cough over the following couple of days and he lived until 2017. In my experience, good news is rarely delivered in a small hospital meeting room.

The paediatric consultant on that day was a very kind female doctor who was overseeing Tom's case. We went in to sit on the couch. I can't remember if there were other people in the room. The results from the MRI were back and I thought, wow, that was fast! Must be nothing. But they don't take you to a small room for nothing. The scan found a 5cm mass in the middle of Tom's head between the cerebellum and his brain stem. As the doctor told me about the mass I was very calm. I don't believe I took it in straight away. It was surreal and I thought, well it'll be something they can fix and he'll be ok. She asked if I wanted to see the scans and I said yes, that it might help with my understanding of what was going on.

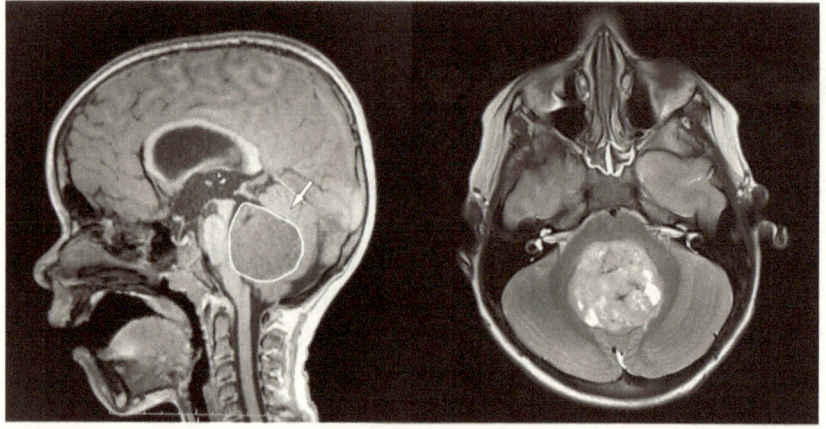

Images taken from MRI brain scan of Thomas, 9th December, 2017

When I saw the screen, I thought that Tom's tumour was just another section of his brain – knowing nothing about anatomy, I hadn't ever seen a brain tumour before. My disbelief was numbing me to the reality of this revelation. My horror at the tumour's size and how far into the middle of his brain it was had me very scared all of a sudden but I wasn't processing it in real time. We went back to the small room and the doctor said I was taking it all very well. Within a minute or two, I broke down. I cried and cried. I started to feel an overwhelming tension in every muscle in my body and I began to shake uncontrollably. Owen was called in to sit with me and I cried some more. I couldn't go out to see Tom in this state but I just wanted to rush to him and climb into bed. I didn't know how I could face him and not have every fear written on my face. I was assured that he was having a wonderful time with the policemen. Playing with the car sirens, handcuffing nurses, a world of novelty to distract him from my absence. I eventually made it out to see Tom and plastered a big smile on my face and tried to act as normally as I could. My heart was beating unnaturally fast. Tom still had his cannula in his right hand but he also had a happy smile on his face with lots of stories to tell. With him happily settled with lots of attention and a TV of his own to control, I headed into the next small room.

The neurosurgical registrar's job was to give me the run down on a treatment plan for the two issues affecting Tom. The first was *hydrocephalus*. The tumour had grown to such a point that the ventricles were unable to drain and the blocked flow of Tom's cerebral-spinal fluid was putting pressure on his brain (see Appendix 1 for further detail). The build-up of this cerebral-spinal fluid was the cause of Tom's exhaustion, headaches and the other new symptoms that had started to manifest themselves. This was the first hurdle to face and we were in crisis mode to address this condition.

I was trying very hard to be sure and clear about every detail that the registrar was telling me. I felt that if I misunderstood, something terrible would happen, so I was very focused on our conversation. There was an element of excitement in the surgeon's face and voice as he told me about the first surgery. He wasn't calm or sombre – in fact, it felt like he was super keen to get in there and rack up some more hours at the table. When he was listing the risks of the operation and what would follow, he explained in a perfectly upbeat voice that infection would be catastrophic. I leaned into Owen and said quietly, "I don't like the word catastrophic," to which the surgeon replied, "but I am just being honest". The bedside manner of this very scary conversation had taken on an almost surreal quality, that the doctor was so 'up' in the delivery of such disastrous news, all while I was still trying to fathom that my little boy needed surgery at all. That morning he was swimming without a care in the world but within 12 hours, he would be on an operating table for brain surgery.

That night, Thomas would undergo a procedure to release the pressure on his brain and have an external ventricle drain (EVD) inserted to keep the cerebral-spinal fluid flowing from his ventricles. I was told that this surgery was 'bread and butter' for neurosurgeons – a fairly common procedure and he would soon be back in Recovery. Tom hadn't eaten all day as there had been a chance of surgery and therefore anaesthetic. He was sitting there in his white and orange striped shirt he'd changed into after swimming and my job was to keep him entertained. To keep him happy while I had just signed a form consenting to the operation which listed that the worst outcome would be…death.

That evening, I said to him that we were going on a ride in his exciting 'bed with wheels' to a new room. That the doctors were going to try to figure out what to do about his tiredness and headaches while he had a sleep. Some sleepy medicine would mean he didn't have to worry about the doctors…and it was past his bedtime. He was so over the day and luckily he didn't question too much. He'd followed all instructions throughout the whole process and everyone was saying how wonderful he was. To this day I don't know if he understood how serious things were right then. I did my best to hide it. All day I had been telling him how proud I was, how much I loved him. These were words he'd heard before but perhaps not as frequently in a regular day, so he may not have considered this to be a red flag that his mum was scared. Perhaps he knew very well that I was scared, but for me, he didn't let on.

After he was given his anaesthetic and he was wheeled away from me I said once more, "I love you Tom-Tom". I didn't say goodbye. I didn't warn him of what was to come. He trusted me completely and I stood there in a nervous state of tension that wouldn't let up as I watched him go. I asked the surgeons to do their very best work, A+ work please. They promised me they would look after him and not to worry. I didn't know at this point the devastating impact the coming surgeries would have on my baby boy.

Once the operation was over, Tom was moved to Recovery. The doctors said that everything went well so with all signs stable, they took Thomas up to Ward 11A – the Neurology ward. There was a drainage tube stitched into his head that led to a bag hanging on a pole. The height of the bag and of Tom's head had to be kept at a constant level so he couldn't get up or move without us considering this drain. He still wore the same orange and white striped t-shirt from the day before. Tom had a shaved section of his head, but I don't think he realised.

The next morning Tom was finally able to eat. We put on a huge feast of anything he wanted – nuggets, pancakes, chips, ice cream, the list went on. The nurses didn't suggest we hold back even though I know they had visions of it all coming back up in one big hurl. He was smiling and back to his old self. Tom still had a cannula in his hand so he was unable to suck his thumb, but he was enthralled by new TV shows he'd not seen before, so he didn't seem to mind too much. My tension wasn't completely gone but I was finding it easier to keep a smile in place for him.

At some point in the following days, a lovely oncologist came to see me about Tom's tumour. Dr Steve said he would be in touch again after the tumour was out and the lab work came back detailing what it was. I was very keen never to see this man again. If it wasn't cancer, we didn't need him. My son didn't have cancer, surely. The mass had to be something else or even if it was – once they got it out, we would be back to normal… surely. I was determined that Tom didn't have cancer.

This was all happening in December. Christmas holidays. Hospital staff coming and going on scheduled leave. We'd meet someone assigned to our team and then their replacement would arrive and back and forward we'd go again. The social workers were keen to give me information on charitable funding and kept delivering hampers from Redkite, the Smith Family, etc. I also had my community of friends and family gathering around asking for ways to help. Many asked to see Tom but I kept it to just close family. I was still in crisis mode. I wasn't interested in assigning jobs or eating Christmas pudding – I just wanted my baby to come home with me. I wanted us to be home by Christmas. I listened over and over to a beautiful, soft song that became a chant in my head. **"Home"** by Ben Abraham is about friends that are off travelling and the singer is calling for their return. It's a soft ballad saying that there are things back here to show them. I tend to find moments and phrases in songs that I grab on to – I always have. The chorus of this song simply repeats the question, "Will you come home?" Sometimes I would sing along, and it would make me cry, but then other times I would change the words to "When you come home". I sang this version to Tom while he slept. This was my hope.

We were in a shared room called the 'Close Obs' room where two nurses were constantly on hand in the room with us. Four ward beds separated by curtains. Four child patients, four families, four different diagnoses. It was full and noisy most of the time. Who would have thought I would feel so alone amidst the chaos of that room, but I did. My only solace was when Tom was awake and chatting with me. Even if he was watching TV, I couldn't get enough of looking at his face. Not since he'd been born had I been as fixated on his every word and movement as in those first few days after December 9th.

I had my phone out a fair bit to video Tom. I remembered his other procedures for his tonsils and his dental work when he'd had a general anaesthetic. Waking up from these were always pretty hilarious. After the external ventricle drain operation, Tom was on some pretty serious pain medication. He would play up to the camera, demanding pizza, refusing laxative juice and watching TV all the while super high on oxycodone. All inhibitions gone, these videos were moments of levity, of laughter and joy in a time of fear – at least for me. Doped up Tom couldn't stay this way for long though and a plan had to be made for our next steps.

Within four days Thomas would be back in theatre, with a specially chosen surgical team whose aim was to remove the mass nestled deep in his brain, past the cerebellum and adjacent to his brain stem. The neurosurgeon came to see us once in the days before Tom's procedure. He was an older man, a bit gruff but professional and to the point. It was late at night and he was tired from what I imagine was a long day. I wish I had asked him then for the process of the surgery and perhaps a million other questions, but I didn't have every question ready and in reality, it didn't matter how he was going to do it. It's not like I could have suggested a better plan. This was just a brief introductory meeting he was having with strangers on his way home.

The next day I decided to speak to the 'ever eager' neurology registrar who had talked with us initially about the external ventricle drain procedure. I asked him to describe what would happen in the surgery. Again, he had a measure of excitement in his eye as he described the steps the operation would take, from incisions to bone saws and retracting Tom's cerebellum which would allow access to the tumour site. With every moment of his enthusiasm, a great exhaustion washed over me and eventually I didn't want to hear anymore. I didn't want to imagine the process. The horror of it all was too much to comprehend anyway. I just felt it was a question that I should ask. As always, the doctors went through all of the possible side effects with us. I look back now and think, surely they didn't tell me everything. Maybe they did and I didn't hear it. It wasn't like I could say no. Tom's chances of survival were dependent on this surgery. A pretty clear choice, so we signed the form.

It was Day 4 - a Wednesday, and Thomas was due in surgery that afternoon. A final MRI had been scheduled for the most up-to-date scans to inform the surgeons that morning and then…he went in. They weren't sure how long it would take until the operation would be finished, but it would be at least a few hours. We were told to go take a walk, get out of the hospital, have a break – they would let us know. My mum, my sisters – Steph, Felicity and Josey – Owen and I headed to Felicity's place down the road to have a lasagne lunch. A glass of wine did little to settle my nerves. My eyes were constantly on my phone and I didn't want to be too far away when the phone call came. We headed back to the hospital and decided to wait upstairs at the fifth floor garden, where we played a board game in the breeze and I tried to keep my thoughts on the turn of play. Normally I'm pretty competitive with my sisters but found myself completely apathetic to the outcome. I was constantly distracted, but it was lovely to have a chance to laugh and have my family around me again. My closest school friend Danielle, a woman I've known for thirty years, arrived while we were waiting. Dan is a nurse practitioner and I knew I could trust her advice around all things medical and what to expect. She joined our little garden group and we sat and chatted, mostly about anything other than what was happening down on Level 4.

My bodily tension had been building for hours and I had been gripping my phone with immense force for some time. It had been five hours since the start of the operation and still no word had come through. It was almost six hours by the time the phone call came. I was still surprised that the surgeon had said he would call me with the outcome, rather than sharing the news in person. I had envisioned another small room, but instead I took a call standing in a corner of the fifth floor garden. My phone rang and I ran across the garden away from my family and friends. I needed to concentrate. I needed to hear everything perfectly clearly. This was the most important conversation I had ever had. Every muscle in my body was frozen in expectation, hope and fear – all at once.

Thomas had survived and was in Recovery. The surgeon had removed all of the tumour. It was out! Or at least 99.99% was out. The procedure took longer than expected as the neurosurgeon had been constantly managing the bleeding from the tumour site. He'd been taking two steps forward and one step back. But all of this was good news. The doctor even said to me that there was a chance it was benign. I nearly fainted at this news. How exhilarating! Surely doctors don't say that to mum's unless it's true. Every single thing he told me was brilliant news and I thought, finally, we have had some good luck. I started to cry and thank him profusely to which the doctor responded with a gruff, "Well, yes, I suggest you gather yourself and be down at Recovery in about an hour". And that was it. The call was over, and my baby was going to be fine!

For most of my adult life, when seeing my loved ones in pain or in hospital, I experience something I call a 'heart pinch'. It's a phrase I made up to describe a brief feeling of sharp pain in my chest directly related to something I had seen. I used to get it when my dad was sick from his heart condition. The biggest one I remember was when I saw my father after his quadruple bypass. I was about 18 years old and dressed up to go to a party with some work friends. I stopped at the hospital on my way and found Dad was in the Intensive Care Unit after surgery. I had never seen my father in such a state. He'd had a dozen procedures over the previous six years but nothing like this. Enormous tubes coming out of his front, bandages on his arms and legs from vein grafts and no colour in his face. My dad had been a farmer, a civil engineer and worked in construction. His face was usually ruddy and brown from the sun. That heart pinch was so intense it took my breath away. I wasn't prepared for how scary it all was in that moment and my glittery top and new jeans made me feel ashamed and ridiculous.

The heart pinch I felt when I first saw Thomas that Wednesday evening was overwhelming and ruinous. Tom didn't stay in Recovery after surgery – instead he was sent to the Paediatric Intensive Care Unit. I couldn't breathe and the stabbing pain in my chest stayed with me for what seemed like an eternity. My eyes filled with tears and I whimpered like a broken bird. At least my boy didn't see. He was still asleep, intubated and covered with monitors and tubes all across his torso and arms. I remember with surreal clarity that a Santa Claus arrived while we were there, offering to come in for a visit. I have no idea why, but they took photos with Tom and then went on their 'merry' way. I realised that we hadn't made it to the shops for our yearly Christmas photo on Santa's knee yet. Tom had just had his Santa photo and didn't know it. Strange, the thoughts that float through your head as you feel the distress of your child in a Paediatric Intensive Care Unit room.

It took Tom quite a while to wake up from his surgery and for his breathing to regulate before it was safe to remove his breathing tube. He was not fully awake, was very drowsy and would float in and out of consciousness. It was a relief though that there was a nurse sitting by him every second, watching his every stat, keeping him comfortable and ready to reassure me that he was doing well.

A few days after we returned to the Close Obs room in 11A, we got a visit from that kind man from oncology – Dr Steve. I felt like saying to him, I don't think you need to see us, the surgeon said it was probably benign, but I didn't get the chance. He was there to tell me that Tom's tumour was cancer and it was malignant. This did not sink in right away. I was still on my 'benign' bandwagon of hope. Interesting that there was no small room for this news – instead we were huddled together, whispering at the end of Tom's hospital bed. Dr Steve had this look on his face. I grew to understand what sort of conversation this look pre-empted. Dr Steve, a gently spoken man with dark hair and thick-rimmed glasses. He usually wore colourful checked shirts and a friendly smile, but his 'small room' face did not present with a smile. His lips would tighten and fall into a frown. His brow would furrow, lines appearing between his eyebrows and his eyes would darken in seriousness. This is when I heard about *medulloblastoma*.

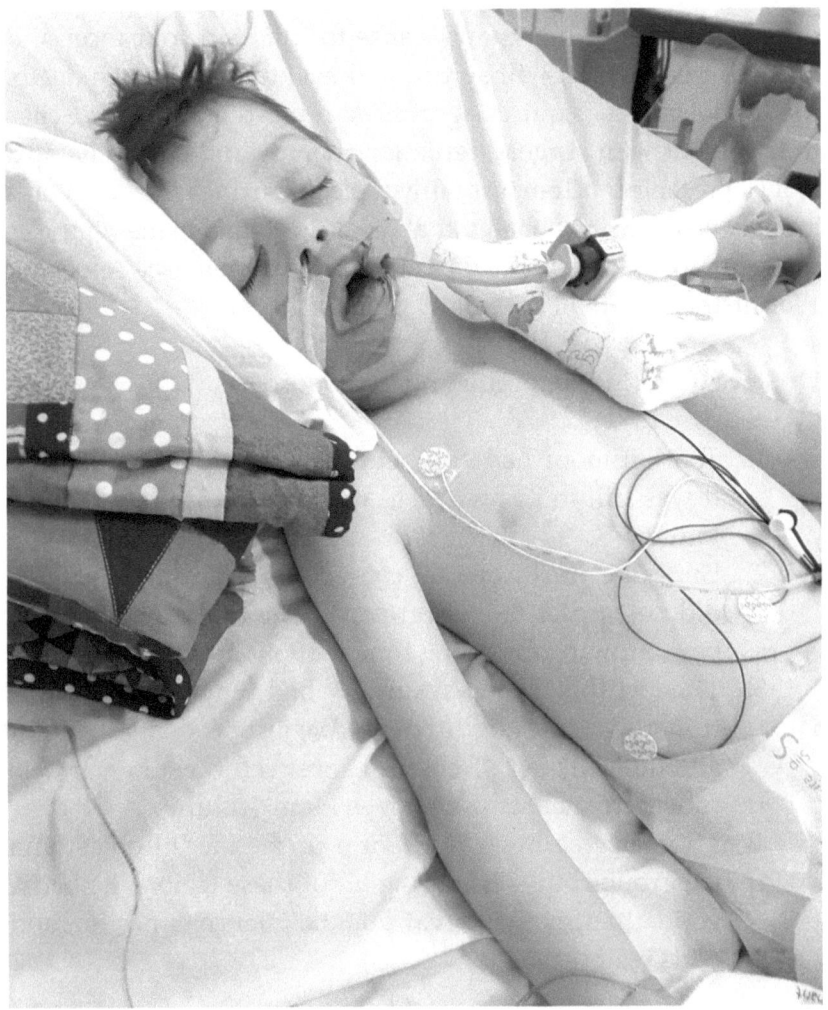

*Thomas – postoperative condition in
Paediatric Intensive Care Unit (PICU)*

Medulloblastoma is the most common paediatric brain malignancy, and accounts for approximately 20% of all paediatric brain tumours. The incidence has been estimated at 1 child in every 200,000 under the age of 15. It occurs in young children often between the ages of 1-10 but can present in teenagers and adults. Boys have a slightly higher rate of occurrence than girls. For the majority of patients, there is no known cause for this type of cancer and without treatment, it will spread and eventually result in death. Medulloblastoma requires aggressive multi-therapy approaches to treatment with surgery, radiation therapy and chemotherapy. How it presented in Tom was fairly typical, starting with symptoms brought on by hydrocephalus (that build-up of fluid in the ventricles of the brain) and the expected location of the tumour (see Appendix 1 for further detail on medulloblastoma).

Dr Steve did bring some good news though:

1) Tom's tumour had not metastasised before we found it. It was still in its own 'egg' with no other tumours to be found.
2) Under the microscope, the cancer cells taken during surgery did not appear to be aggressive. The tumour could have been growing for a long time without us noticing.
3) The fact that Thomas' surgery had removed the whole tumour was wonderful news. We just needed to treat for any little bits left. Even one cancer cell was too many, so cancer treatments were now in Tom's future.
4) Thomas was in Group 3 or 4 of the medulloblastoma subgroups but considering all of these factors, he had a good chance of survival. 70-80% chance is pretty good odds really.

Later that week, a decision about a final surgery would have to be made. The doctors needed to test Tom's external ventricle drain. That was the tube connected to a bag leaking out cerebral-spinal fluid. I tried to explain this to a friend. Tom's head and bag needed to be level when the drain was open. They actually used a spirit level on a string to measure how high on the pole the bag needed to be. I said, we are hoping his fluid will stop looking so much like a rosé and more like vodka. The idea was that once the tumour was gone, Tom's cerebral-spinal fluid would be able to naturally drain through his brain and down his spine and not require any assistance. The blockage was gone now so it made sense.

Instead, the wound site started to leak, and Tom was then in higher danger of infection. The neurology team informed us that a shunt would be needed – an internal drain that would assist in emptying Tom's ventricles but something which he would have in his head forever (see Appendix 1 for further information about shunts). It wasn't ideal but it wasn't the worst thing to happen. My boy was alive and tumour-free. After the shunt procedure, we were moved into a private room and continued on our long road of recovery. We weren't prepared for what was to come next.

Practical Advice:

- Try to not take it personally if doctors don't deliver information in the way you would expect or prefer.

- Don't forget to eat regularly and have something warm to throw on – hospitals are always so cold.

- It's ok to ask questions, more than once if it doesn't sink in.

- Write stuff down if you know you'll forget it. Have the doctors write down tricky 'medi-speak' if it will help.

- In Australia, treatment for childhood cancer is financially covered by the government. This includes hospital stays, all surgeries, therapies, oncology treatments, imaging, education, equipment, and so on. The only costs we paid were outpatient medications which were capped at $6.40 per prescription. It is difficult to consider dealing with welfare options when you are amidst all of this but if you can, apply for whatever carer payments you can with Centrelink or whatever social services are available to you. Do this early on as this might also allow you to access your superfund down the track when you are running low on money for everyday expenses while you are off work.

- <u>For supporters of parents:</u> Coordinate with a family member to deliver care packages/food to your people. Your friend may not want to be fielding phone calls.

- <u>For co-parenting families:</u> Find a family counsellor early on into a diagnosis like this. Someone both parents like and trust. Having a mediator along the way is helpful when stressful times require big decisions.

Chapter 2

Back to Square One

Posterior Fossa Syndrome

There were so many conversations with doctors during our time in hospital about possible risks and side effects from treatment options. A number of the discussions around Tom's three neurosurgeries were focused on anaesthetic and why we had to do it. The doctors explained the external ventricle drain and the shunt procedures as being very common neurosurgery, nothing to really worry about. 'Bread and butter' for a neurosurgeon I was told. For Tom these went well, and I probably didn't have to worry as much as I did. It was the tumour surgery that was both the greatest danger and hope for Tom.

The reason to operate was undeniable and essential to Tom's survival. The tumour had to come out. So the positives were clear, and the list of risks were really more warnings than providing an option to refuse the procedure. The registrar did say to me that as a consequence of the surgery, Tom would most likely experience *cerebellar mutism* afterwards due to the surgical path through which the surgeon would need to access the tumour – i.e. through the cerebellum. He assured me that Tom's speech would return but this was a common side effect of the operation. Also, a side effect of the steroids used for swelling and the trauma of the procedure in general would likely mean that Tom would be 'cranky' once he woke.

The doctors also mentioned that some patients will experience *posterior fossa syndrome* (PFS). I don't recall the full impact of this particular syndrome ever being completely outlined to me – perhaps because it doesn't eventuate in all patients and there was no need to go into detail? I remember the repeated side effects listed to me were 'mute and cranky'. I could handle 'mute and cranky' if it meant Tom survived the surgery. I was fine with 'mute and cranky' if they could get the whole tumour out. Every surgery Tom underwent had the very real possibility of stroke or death as the outcome so a temporary phase of 'mute and cranky' was a very acceptable condition to me.

Tom was very slow to regain consciousness after his tumour resection surgery. He had extended time in the Paediatric Intensive Care Unit and then he was back into the Close Obs ward room. When he woke, we did not just see 'mute and cranky'. It was so much more devastating than that. The doctors described Tom's behaviour as 'agitation,' but that term is still a grossly inadequate description. When Tom wasn't in long periods of unconsciousness, he was screaming and thrashing in the bed. His thin arms were so over stretched I thought his elbows would pop backwards and his legs would surely cramp through strain. The doctors called this 'posturing'. We quickly learned to surround him in pillows, eventually known as the 'pillow palace', to ensure Tom didn't hurt himself in his violent flailing. I would attempt to restrain him with hugs and try to fold his arms back away from their over-extension.

Tom had acquired an extremely severe brain injury known as posterior fossa syndrome (see Appendix 2 for general detail on this syndrome) that took away his ability to control any voluntary muscle movement. His eyes were unfocused, only one of them straight and they would roll back in his head which to me looked like he was in great pain. He could no longer balance to sit or stand, move his fingers, or follow any direction of the medical staff. He had *dysphagia* which meant he could no longer swallow. Before surgery, I wasn't to know he'd had his last meal for the next 8-9 months. He had cannulas in his hands and feet, a catheter, a nasogastric tube as well as the draining tube exiting his skull. I was grateful that at least he was still able to breathe on his own. My distress was immense and there was nothing I could do to fix it for him. These were all necessary evils that my bub had to endure as a result of getting the tumour out of his head.

The neurology team wasn't really able to help with any of this but the nursing staff in the ward were familiar with how this syndrome could play out. They were ready for the screaming. I doubt the rest of the families in that room were. After a day or two, Dr Steve came to visit. He'd heard about Tom's distress and came to advise. I hated to see my boy in pain but there were some other possibilities. Dr Steve explained that Tom's agitation could have been borne of a number of factors, such as:

- The impact of the steroids
- Frustration with not being able to communicate
- His uncontrolled movements might have been his brain trying to find his muscles but without control or nuance
- He might have just wanted to go to the toilet at times but his only way of communicating was in a scream because his speech was gone
- It could have been in reaction to pain.

The doctors increased Tom's pain medication but there was a close watch given to bowel movements considering these drugs tend to block you up. Tom needed a number of further drugs to get his bowels started again when a week passed with no sign of a No. 2. The doctors were cautious not to overmedicate his pain because it would be more difficult to understand the full impact of his brain injury if he was always sedated. The doctors had to know if there were issues that needed resolving through further surgery. They needed to see his faculties return and to what degree. So, after a couple of weeks the doctors reduced his medication alongside some other strategies.

Tom's shunt operation happened a week after his tumour operation – Day 11. His return to Ward 11A saw us in a huge private room. The chaos of the Close Obs room was behind us now that the drain was out, and we could set the conditions. The room was always dark and quiet. We tried a lot of other things to calm him like massaging him in long strokes and putting on some music. As a music teacher, I've always had a special relationship with music. It sorts me out when I need to process something, when I'm emotional, when I need a kick start. Most of the time I have music in my head. I went back to my tried and tested techniques from when the boys were babies. 'Sirens' by Ben Abraham was an album I used to listen to when I was going through tough times a few years before all of this happened. I noticed that the boys would always be lulled to sleep by it when we went anywhere in the car. This particular songwriter had such a beautiful warmth in his voice, and it would put them in a trance. I would sing along, and the songs would calm me too.

The song **"I Belong To You"** was particularly evocative to me at this time. It embodied my helplessness, my worry over how best to help Tom. The second verse called out my fear of knowing more about the stakes than I was telling my boy. The third verse spoke to me of hope. Hope that whatever I was doing was going to bring him back to me. These songs saved me so many times in that room kneeling over Tom. I'd be there for what seemed like an eternity patting him on the bum to help him find some calm. He also liked a bit of instrumental acoustic guitar and even the sound of rain.

One other thing that would sometimes work was to just hold him and softly shush him back to sleep. All the way through the journey when things were too much, this was my go-to. Picking him up or climbing into bed for a Mummy cuddle was an effective plan. It also was good for me too. I think we helped each other most of the time. Nothing was a guarantee though and when everything failed, a nurse said to me once, "Sometimes, not doing anything can be the best option". And sometimes Tom did calm himself and probably wanted some space from all the hovering and 'helping'.

I know what didn't help – telling Tom to stop crying. Talking reason, asking him to stop screaming. I was so frantic in myself for it to stop; for him, but also for my sake. My legs would lock up as I knelt on the bed for long sessions. My back constantly felt broken from crouching over him. My soul was being ripped from me with every scream. I remember looking around the room on a particularly bad night seeing my mum and Owen watching on in despair. I know I had this look of fear and desperation in my eyes. But they were as helpless as me. I didn't know when it was going to get better and again, I couldn't fix it. This perhaps was the biggest demon I was fighting – the helplessness that came with watching him suffer. I'll never forget those torturous weeks leading up to Christmas but thankfully Tom did.

Time and again, I thought – why didn't anyone tell us this would happen? Was this a surprise to them as well? All of the 'wins' we had at the end of the surgery: alive, tumour out, possibly benign… these were quickly out of my mind with what seemed like a far worse alternative. Suffice to say, we kept Cameron, Tom's twin brother, well away from the hospital room as much as possible. There were times when even adult visitors struggled with Tom's episodes of agitation and so we tried to protect Cam as much as we could. I'm sure the separation affected him to a certain extent, but it was school holidays, so it was a calendar filled with playdates, time with my mum, aka: Nanna and of course… time with us, when we were on a break from the ward. The fact was that even in the coming months, Tom was so different to how Cam knew his brother, so he only came for very short visits.

In talking to Dr Steve and other allied health specialists, it seemed that Tom's severity of *posterior fossa syndrome* was quite extreme. Most children end up with a temporary version of 'mute and cranky' but Tom's presentation was far more complex. There isn't any comprehensive understanding of why some kids experience this and some don't (see Appendix 2 for more detail on posterior fossa syndrome and cerebellar mutism). We came to realise that Tom was going to require extensive and long-term rehabilitation which would happen alongside his cancer treatments and beyond.

Sometime after Christmas we were past the worst as Tom's agitation abated and he settled down into his new life in hospital. We stayed in Ward 11A for five weeks in total before we were moved to the Rehabilitation Ward – 8A. I was overwhelmed a lot of the time in 11A, tired all of the time as well as being in a constant state of confusion, anxiety and fear. The boys' birthday is in January and so when their 7th birthday came up and we still had a long way to go, I remember how miserable I was that I couldn't give the boys their annual party. Cam came up to the hospital and had a photo with Tom. This was no birthday for Tom – not as he knew birthdays. Birthdays were games and friends and homemade cakes and the sugar coma that always followed.

Even though I knew treatment for his cancer was on the horizon, we began to focus on rehabilitating Tom's brain injury in the months that followed. Hayley, our wonderful physiotherapist, brought us his new wheelchair with head support and a good range of tilt so we could finally get Tom out of his bed. Tom was still unable to sit or even hold his head up but now with our new wheels we could go get some fresh air. I thought the change of scenery, new sounds, no more beeping machines would be great so one day we headed for the fifth floor garden. Tom wasn't as impressed with his new chair as we'd hoped, but little sessions sitting up were on the rehab checklist so off we went. As we took the elevator downstairs Tom started to get upset. He still couldn't talk so his only way of communicating was to scream and cry. I wheeled him past all of the people waiting for the Oncology Day clinic on Level 5 and my heart was breaking. Tom's cries, his contorted face and his mouth still constantly secreting saliva made for a very difficult sight. I watched people stare, I watched them turn away. I felt for the first time how intensely we had been in our own little bubble, but outside that room, Tom's battle was confronting for the world to see. Once we got to the garden, I joined Tom in his distress, and we had a cry together. Our first excursion was something of a failure, but we would try and try again.

Another thing that was a struggle for Tom was controlling his face. He was constantly trying to talk and didn't understand why he couldn't find his voice. He also had difficulty opening his eyes, closing his mouth and controlling other facial muscles. Remember he couldn't swallow and if you think about how often you swallow, even when not eating, we found that we were constantly dealing with saliva secretions. In other words, for a long time he was constantly in a state of drool. Life became a mission of managing Tom's vomiting and his secretions. Towels, vomit bags, soft paper towels for spit. Sometimes every few minutes I would be wiping away spit. Because of this, Tom's lips suffered. Regardless of the paraffin wax the nurses suggested I applied, his lips would peel away and sometimes be left bleeding and scabbing due to the constant assault of 'the wipe'.

A set of big achievements came when Tom was able to retract his tongue, as it would often sit out, as well as when he learnt to close his mouth and when he learnt to spit. So eventually the uncontrolled secretions started to become easier to deal with, but they would still continue to be an issue until Tom would learn to swallow. I have so many photos of Tom with 'spit towels' chocked under his cheek to catch the wet. We would clean out his mouth with little pink sponges to freshen his mouth up since he was not allowed anything to eat or drink.

Tom had always been a tactile boy. He would run the back of his hand over the pillowcase when he was falling asleep. He sucked his thumb from infancy, he was always fiddling with something. From when the boys were toddlers, we had started a little ritual when one of us needed help or if we were upset. We'd put our hand out, fingers wide and say, "big hand, little hand". This meant that we would stretch out one hand to each other and our fingers would intertwine, and we would squeeze. Sometimes I would fold my thumb in and tickle his palm. I almost always got a smile and a giggle. Cameron seemed to need it less and less as he got older, so it became a thing between Tom and I. Every four hours the nurses would come in to do observations on Tom. Blood pressure, a light in the eyes, temperature and the like – also known as 'obs', or doing numbers, 'gotta check your muscles Tom' and other such euphemisms. There was physical data to check and record but also neurological observations. Since the first operation in December, one of the first questions the nurses would ask Tom was, "Can you squeeze my hand Tom?" This one always stood out to me. I would always try our 'big hand, little hand' to see if he would squeeze for me but for so long it didn't work. Then one day in February, it did. I cried like a baby.

In the broad scheme of things perhaps a hand squeeze was small, but it was a first and it was exciting. Tom's brain needed to rediscover every pathway to every muscle in his body. Even when he would find that muscle, he had to keep practicing and find it again and again until it eventually took less energy and concentration for him. At first his movements were crude and large, without nuance. Control was also something he would have to learn. For example, Tom had to work hard and think hard about stretching his fingers from a clenched fist. In the past, if he wanted to, he could do so instantaneously. But now, every movement was a momentous challenge.

The Occupational Therapist, Physiotherapist and Speech Therapist in the Oncology and Neurology departments were amazing. One day they left a little gold-coloured egg shaker with us. I would sit the egg in Tom's palm and ask him to tip it out or 'throw the egg'. At first, it stayed in Tom's hand for a long time and so I would carefully tilt his hand for it to fall. I would do this over and over. Then I would ask Tom to try. It might have taken him five minutes of concentration. Five minutes of his elbow moving but not his hand. Five minutes where at the end he was so frustrated he would start to cry. Five minutes of work, but then he got it. He tilted his hand and he 'threw' the egg. We kept working and working on this until we got it down to one minute, then to 20 seconds, then 10 seconds until finally he could do it on command. Another awesome milestone which took us weeks to build. This first step led to throwing his hand onto mine and then to another task of pulling a medication syringe out of itself. This trick was pretty amazing as it took coordination between his hands, strength from his arms and fingers around the tube. Things were coming back quicker as the months passed.

Tom's ability to hear never seemed to be affected by his posterior fossa or the surgery and so I felt that my voice and music were ways to help him and communicate, even if he couldn't respond as he wanted to. His ability to see and focus was gone initially but slowly improved over the first couple of months or so. Tom would often keep his eyes shut when it was too bright (particularly outside) but over time, his eye control returned. He now had hearing and sight – two tools that he could use to find us again and make sense of what was going on. So, once he could see, it was time to put on a show. I had family and friends make hand puppets of different characters and I would put on funny voices to commentate, tell stories and joke around with. As funny as I was at these little puppet shows, my sister, Steph was always the best – she always knew the best line of chat for each character that got Tom smiling.

An inventory of this stable of puppet friends was as follows: There was Dr Feelgood who sounded like an African-American Disco Stu type guy – he liked to break into song. There was a dog 'Spot', a little boy, a little girl and a little old lady named Pearl. Importantly, there was

Mary Margaret, an older Scottish lady with a strict sense of propriety. She was all mine and the most fun to have jokes with about poos, wees and the ever-popular fart humour – the perfect joke topic for a seven-year-old boy. This character had been with us for years – I would break out into my accent and get all ridiculous at random times, usually in the car or making dinner. The accent cracked the boys up and we all had a good laugh at the stern lady who would be telling them what for! It became my favourite pastime of making Tom laugh.

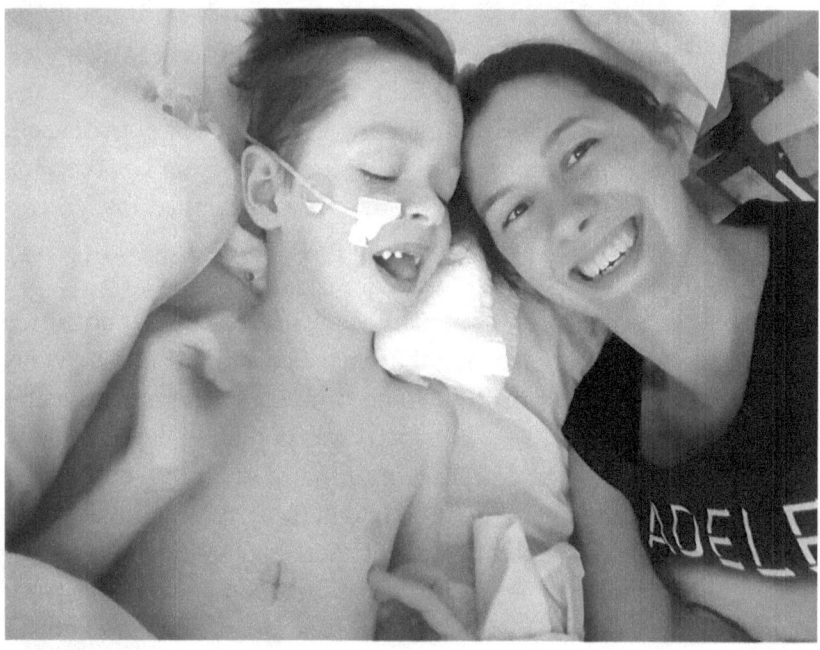

As time rolled on and we started to make small points of progress my devastation turned to determination and I was sure we were going to get there. A good friend of mine suffered a terrible accident a few years prior and I remember someone saying to me, "If it takes a year to come back, it's just a year. One year in a long life is nothing but a blip. A blip that makes you stronger." Even longer than a year was ok if there was hope of finding our way back. This was my mantra along the way. I guess it was a way of looking at it that was bearable and this was my hope.

Practical Advice:

- Try everything until something works.

- Try to keep *your* frantic down and remember that if the parent is calm it's easier for the kids to be calm.

- In the chaotic times, take the opportunity when they sleep to have your quiet time then, to have some food, to get feeling back in your legs, to sleep if possible.

- It might sound trite but if you don't sleep, eat, breathe or just generally cope it's worse for your bub. Patience is harder to find if you are tired. You don't how long this will last so prepare for the marathon.

- Every little achievement is amazing.

- Find ways to get a smile: it always made my day.

- Supporters: If there are siblings that need looking after, offer to take them for a movie or a playdate. Otherwise, send messages of support without expecting or needing a response.

- Co-parents: Try to work out a schedule between the two of you whether it be for 5, 12 or 24 hours. Have handovers like the nurses do and get out of the hospital for a break.

Chapter 3

A New Home

Hospital Life

It became clear after the resection operation that we were going to be settled into hospital life for a long time. Once we were in a big private room we decorated for Christmas; brought in toys and lights and games. The rooms at Lady Cilento Children's Hospital were big, most with a private fridge and in oncology they even had microwaves, so we stocked the fridge and cupboard space. A nurse asked me if I had been taught how to run Tom's feed pump. I didn't think there would be any need for that – Tom would surely be eating again before we went home. Then the nurses started to train me on how to prepare his medications. Again, why would I need to know? He would be better before we left here.

It was through conversations like these that I slowly got the picture that life in the long term was going to be quite different. Tom's altered state was going to take time in terms of recovery and rehabilitation. It would change our lives and it would change me. I was going to become his nurse, his therapist and his advocate in ways far more meaningful than I had ever been before. So in Neurology I learnt how to work his pump. In Rehabilitation I learned to prepare his meds. This meant crushing tablets, dissolving them, drawing up correct doses with a syringe and then administering them. Every ward after that I changed his feeds over. For this, I needed to draw up fluid from Tom's stomach, check the PH levels and if we were sure the tube was clearly sitting in the right place, I would start his feed. Tom's nausea and constant vomiting throughout his illness meant that his nutritionist would work with us experimenting with bolus (hours on and hours off food) or continuous feed options. Some of the many lessons to become a new version of a mum for a new version of my Tom.

Over the many months Tom was an inpatient, we bounced wards. We would sometimes only get 20 minutes notice for a room change, which usually meant a ward change as well. Between the Paediatric Intensive Care Unit, Emergency, Oncology, Neurology, Rehabilitation and general medical wards, as well as visits to Radiotherapy, Pharmacy, Audiology, Imaging and Theatre, we saw a lot of the hospital. Beds in oncology were prioritised for kids having chemotherapy and those dealing with neutropenia who were at serious risk of infection. Once we were cleared from the neurology team of doctors we moved to oncology for a short time. A week later we were moved down to the Rehabilitation floor – Ward 8A for a much longer stay.

On level 11 we were used to a high frequency of nurse visits. Constantly checking obs, giving medications, helping us with vomit clean ups and other bits and pieces. Things were far more relaxed in rehab. For most kids going through treatment for cancer, they can do so mostly as outpatients with visits to radiation and some short stays for chemotherapy. Our experience was complicated by Tom's brain injury. He needed to start radiation six weeks after the surgery, but we weren't able to go home yet. It was difficult to transport Tom and as his care needs were still so high, he was unable to go home, and so we stayed.

A NEW HOME

Thomas was still working with his oncology allied health team: Ash (Speech Therapist), Hayley, (Physiotherapist) and Anna (Occupational Therapist). Hayley was in charge of building his strength, stamina, balance and posture. She would come in with all types of equipment. The foam mat for floor work was something Tom actually enjoyed. He had to work hard to get down on the floor but so did we. I think he liked how it was just as difficult for the adults to get down on the ground and roll and stretch and reach for things. The wheelchair was such an important element for Tom's rehabilitation, but he hated it at first. We would have a little bit more chair time each day, until he got used to it. The commode for the shower was not popular with young Tom either. This never changed.

Then the Standing Frame came. Thomas hated that even more. He hadn't put his feet to the floor with any weight for months. The capacity of his feet and legs to bear his own weight had severely deteriorated and he could only stand this way for short periods of time. We would wheel Tom around in his stander and try to distract him from his discomfort and the strange feelings he was having to cope with. To start, a lot of the time when we would walk the halls he would cry and wail. He couldn't open his eyes, he was uncomfortable, scared and was working so hard. After a time, he would go along with us in silence. Eventually he started to laugh. We would pretend that Hayley was a rubbish driver of the stander and she'd softly bump into people and things. Tom liked the idea of a bit of chaos and had a giggle. He had always been a speed demon and loved it when we would set it up so he would chase me down the corridors of the ward. It was such a joy to hear him laugh. The standing frame also became useful for playing ball – practicing the catch and the release. Over weeks of daily time in his chair and his stander Tom was regaining his balance and some strength in his core, legs and arms.

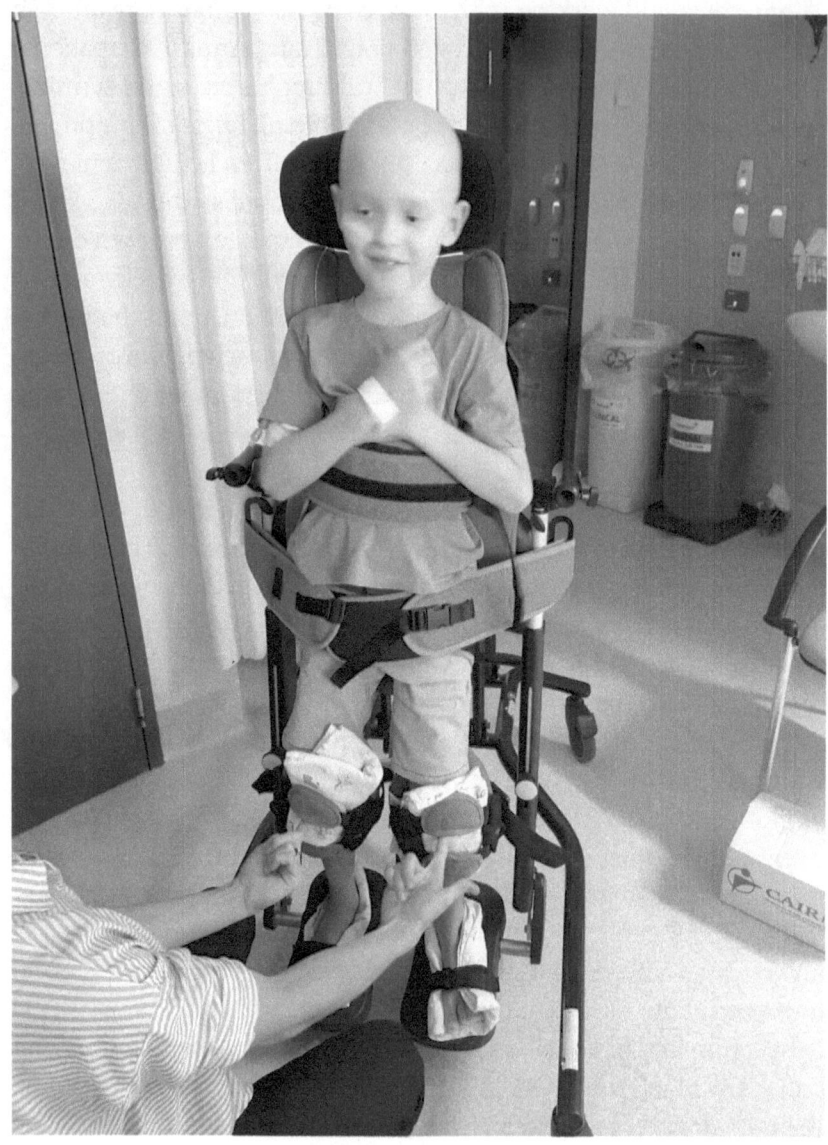

Ash had some very important work to do with Tom's speech and swallowing mechanism. I was desperate to hear my bubba talk again even just to call me Mum, tell me he needed to go to the toilet, be happy or sad or…anything! Speech was our focus and so we used laminated cards for Yes and No. We tried picture cards for him to use his eyes to indicate which option he wanted. We explained and re-explained these visual cues over and over again. It started with his eyes and then his hand and we were able to figure out what he needed. It did make life easier, but I was still hanging out for his voice. To hear him call me Mum. Then one day, in the rehab block between radiation and chemo, Tom spoke. His first new words were 'Bye' and 'Hi'. I wasn't there for it – his dad was on that day. I ran into Tom's new rehab speechie, Georgia, that night at an Ed Sheeran concert. She told me Tom had spoken. He'd hit this amazing new milestone. He'd said 'Bye'. I was ecstatic. Everything was brighter, more dazzling, more colourful that night. My cheeks were sore from smiling and wet from elated tears. I hadn't heard him myself, but the world was so much better now that his voice was coming back. I would hear Tom speak the following day when I was back in his room and we were on the road to having our chats back.

Occupational Therapy focused on Tom's fine motor control which was a harder thing for Tom to get back. Joint sessions with Occupational Therapist Anna and the other therapists made for great games involving lots of toys. It required a lot of concentration from Tom – to figure out which toy to use, where something had to go, how to pick it up and then start again. New games, new toys and we slowly graduated in difficulty as Tom improved bit by bit. Anna and Hayley also worked hard on Tom's capacity to sit and the stamina he needed to even hold his head up for a small amount of time. We would practice in the wheelchair with a little less tilt each time and also on the bathroom commode and finally in a regular chair. One day he finally felt comfortable enough to try the regular chair. Tom looked up at me and smiled. It was early March and another beautiful day in his progress. His time in that chair that day wasn't very long, but he was so proud of himself. He was doing something he used to be able to do.

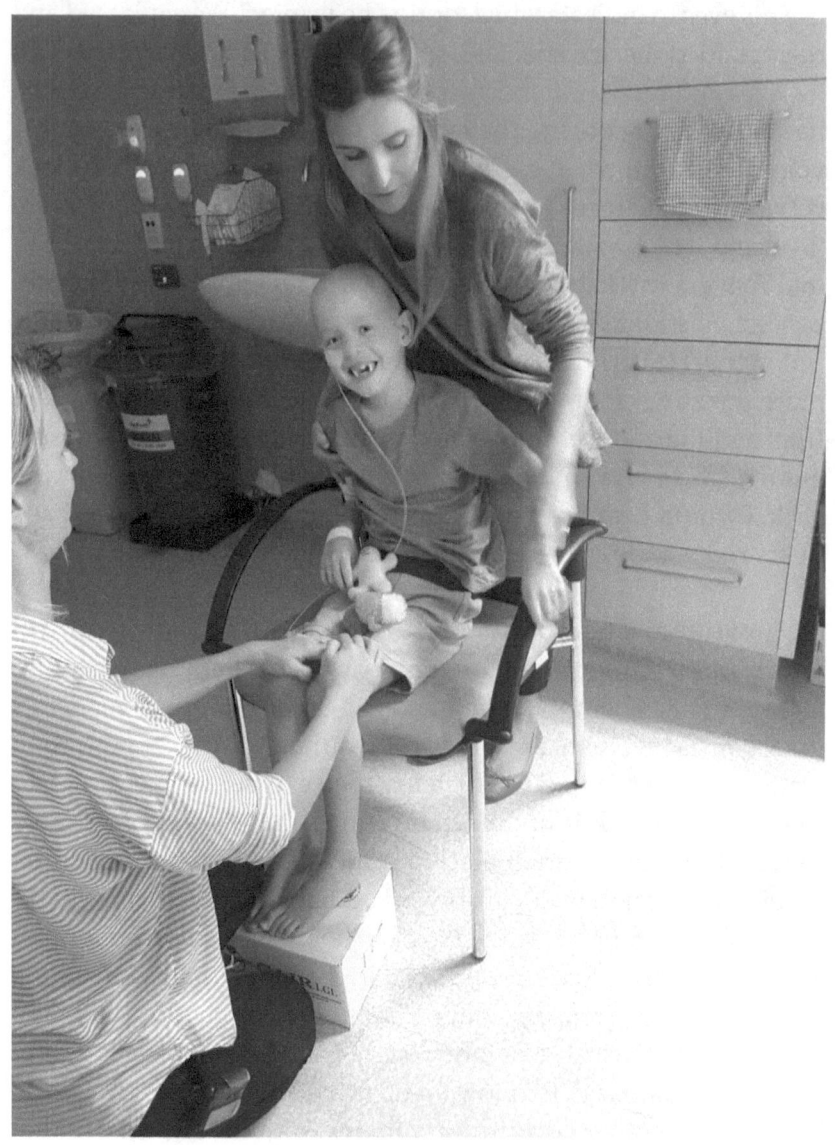

Anna's job was also to check in on Tom's understanding of all that had happened and why. None of us got much warning of the brain injury that came but we had been walked through the implications of the cancer. The trick was to talk to Tom in consistent language he could grasp. I named the tumour 'the egg in your head'. When

A NEW HOME

I looked at the scan, that's exactly what it looked like to me, in both size and shape and so we would talk about the 'egg'. Our conversations went through how we found it, why it had to come out, etc, but I hated that we never had an explanation as to why. "It's just bad luck honey. This wasn't from anything you did; this isn't your fault. It's no one's fault. It's just terrible luck but we have to deal with it because cancer can't stay in someone's body."

After Tom's initial diagnosis, the doctors scheduled an MRI for Cameron. While Dr Steve had assured me that medulloblastoma was not a genetically transferred disease I was still worried. Cam had experienced none of the symptoms Tom had and the MRI results showed Cameron's was clear. I was relieved of course. In my head though, I thought – how does something like this get decided by the gods or science or fate? How does one twin get spared while the other must fight? Throughout 2018, I was constantly struck by the contrast between my two boys. Cam, who could chatter away, jump on the trampoline and learn to ride his new scooter. The time I would spend with Tom was so starkly different and heartbreaking when I would consider the comparison.

As we spoke with Tom about his tumour, it was also important to explain it all to Cameron, particularly as we had shielded Cam from the majority of Tom's difficulties at the start. I remember him almost avoiding the topic most of the time. Cam was worried about the 'egg' being his fault somehow. "What if I knocked Tom's head when we were in your tummy?" he asked repeatedly. He was reassured time and again that it wasn't his fault that Tom had the egg. That he couldn't catch it. That he didn't have it because the pictures we took of his head showed no egg anywhere. Many of his questions came later but at the start I think he preferred not to think too hard about it.

This therapist team and Tom's team of doctors were our main staff visitors as well as our clinical nurse – Brooke. She was to be our case manager of sorts. She would answer any questions, chase up concerns with the doctors, listen to us vent or cry or whatever. I probably needed to use Brooke more often but with only one clinical nurse with so many cases to manage, I didn't see her very much and I didn't think to call her unless it was an emergency. The beautiful teachers from the hospital school would also come up and attempt activities with Thomas at bedside or in his wheelchair. He found it difficult because he couldn't speak very much, write or even control his hands completely. He plodded along with the teachers and us. We would patiently ask him questions to keep him thinking even if he couldn't answer. As his gross motor control improved we would help him move and point to things.

Tom and I really enjoyed the visits from the Music Therapist. As a music teacher, far removed from my classroom, it was so lovely to sing and play with Tom. He was transfixed by the rainbow themed rain stick and usually bashed away at something while we sang and played guitar. Thomas would be asked what music he liked and one of his favourites – which was not on the standard kids' playlist – was **"Thunder"** by Imagine Dragons. Tom struggled to sing along because for a very long time his speech was slow to come out. He would need to breathe between each syllable to start and then might get a few words in a row. He loved this song. He loved to hear any music and over our time in hospital Tom developed his personal playlist which would grow all year. Music was something special to both of us. Sometimes when I listen to the words of this song, I think to myself – Tom was this powerful force of light. He was bright and shining, a flash of energy; he was lightening. His tumour was the thunder that followed him. A grumbling that was in the distance but still in the background of our world.

Lady Cilento Children's Hospital had a number of wonderful people organised to visit the wards. I remember so many superhero and fictional characters in full costume coming along. A lot of the time Thomas was keen to beat them in an arm wrestle. We were called on by army officers, pet therapy volunteers and puppeteers from Camp Quality. Always on hand were the young Captains

A NEW HOME

from Starlight and the Hospital Foundation volunteers ready to play games with Thomas. He had a few favourite games such as 'Trouble', 'Connect Four' and memory card games but after months of playing with me, it was nice for him to play with other people. Tom would teach them how his games were played. He was often the champion which was always a hit. These visitors were important for me too. Apart from garnering such joy and delight on Tom's face, there were times I could step out for a breather, chat with a staff member in private or even just make a phone call. What amazing people there are in the world that spend their time lifting up the spirits of sick children. Our days were made up of these visits and otherwise we had our time together.

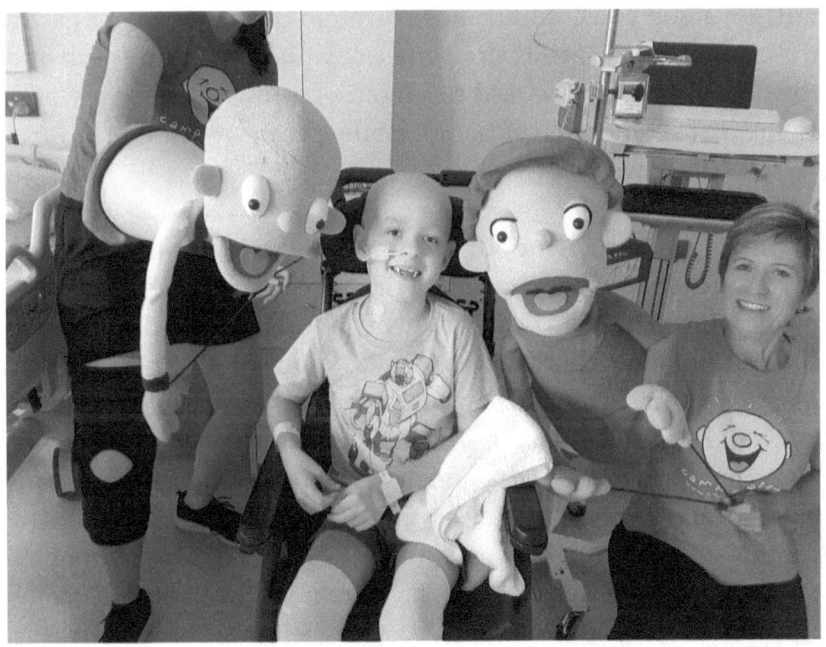

Bedside visits - Camp Quality Puppets

One of my favourite activities with Thomas was to go for our walks. We had an enormous collection of caps to choose from that had been generously gifted to Tom over the summer. He'd pick his hat for the day and we'd be off. The beauty of a walk with Tom was always such an important time for us and I am so thankful for the parklands by the children's hospital. Southbank is quite the landmark in Brisbane, an enormous spread of parkland, restaurants, pools, boardwalks and playgrounds alongside the river. There is a winding pathway under an arbour of pinkish-purple bougainvillea climbers that Tom and I would walk under whenever we could get outside. For half an hour or for half a day on the weekend, Southbank was our place to explore. When I go there now, I see Thomas everywhere. In the summer on a Sunday, there was live music playing on the green. Overlooking the river, we would sit and listen. Tom would practice his claps. Further along you could wander through the markets and get an ice-cream from a cart. Every time we walked past the beach and the pool Tom's hand would reach out pointing to the blue water. In the first six months, although he desperately wanted to swim, he wasn't allowed to.

Thomas needed a 'line' direct into his bloodstream that was surgically embedded to facilitate the anaesthetic and intravenous medications. This tube went into his arm and threaded through into the interior of his chest. It was his 'PIC' line or PICC (peripherally inserted central catheter) and later it would be replaced with a 'central' line which was inserted into the right side of his chest. These lines had to stay clean and dry at all times. No baths or swims allowed, and it was bagged every time I showered him. The dressing for this line had to be changed once a week and didn't Tom hate those days. There was no kind way to remove the tape holding the transparent cover in place and most times Tom would be left with red, stinging skin that was then chemically cleaned before new tape was placed over the still inflamed skin. We tried every distraction possible but it was always such a mission and so uncomfortable and painful for my boy. He would cry and I would hold him still, deceitfully saying "it's okay honey, it'll be okay". But it was never okay. Not for him and not for me but I said it anyway. Thomas got to know which visits to dread pretty quickly. Observations were fine, doctor visits were fine and even x-rays were tolerated. But dressing changes, blood tests, ultrasounds, or anything to do with the Paediatric Intensive Care Unit or surgery were not popular.

Lines and tubes didn't stop our adventures though. If we were out early enough in the morning on a hot day, Tom loved to feel the spray of the sprinklers watering the grass. There is a beautiful green space between the street of restaurants and the arbour walk with a big poinciana tree in the middle. I would lie out a blanket – usually one of the donated quilts from the hospital – and Tom and I would lay down together on the grass and look up at the sky. Floor time was something Tom really enjoyed both in the room and out at the park. He could practice rolling around, lifting himself onto his elbows to just have a break from the chair and have a good stretch. My boys were always skinny and lanky – a genetic inheritance from my mum's side. Consequently, his poor little bum would get sore after a time in the chair regardless of the cushioning or the tilt of the seat.

There was a new light installation at Southbank that opened in April of that year. At dusk before we had to be back for evening meds, we would stop and lie down on the roped beds inside a large cage of lit poles. These poles were lined with changing LED lights that stretched up to join at a circle above our heads. There was calm, meditative-like music playing and as the sun faded away, the lights became more intense and we watched them morph in patterns and form moving rainbows of iridescence on a black sky canvas. To begin with Tom couldn't keep his eyes open for long. The lights were bright and his sensitivity to light was still problematic. But as time passed, he would ask to visit the lights and we would lie down, side by side, looking up. And it was magical.

Southbank boasts a beautiful playground that in times past, Tom and Cam would enjoy for hours. I know Tom struggled with his limitations and watching the other kids play. As time went on and his strength improved, we decided to try little walks near the play equipment. I'd hold him from behind and he would walk. Uneven steps that were awkward and took great effort – but he would walk with my help. The physio department had made Thomas boots also known as Ankle Foot Orthoses. These supported his feet, ankles and calves and stretched up to just below his knees and as an added bonus were decorated with images of Batman. In these Batman Boots, extra stability meant he could walk and even climb but they were heavy and so he needed to build the strength to lift them. Then he was determined to try the ladder. I remember the day he climbed the four-step ladder up to the higher platform. We then walked over to the slide and prepared for the slide down. The larger playground designed for kids of Tom's age was too busy and difficult to attempt so we had chosen the one for smaller children and toddlers. The top of the slide had a border above it that made a circle through which children would push through. I am six foot and I came close to getting stuck when I realised just how narrow the slide itself was. It brought Thomas no end of enjoyment to hear that my bum almost didn't fit. He cackled all the way down as we pushed off together. We had found a new physio activity and he was again finding his way back to the things he had loved before.

Most days we would go on our coffee date. A little coffee shop on the corner where Tom would point to chocolate doughnuts and help me decide between banana bread or bagels. A handful of times I would ask Tom if he would take me to lunch. He enjoyed the pub called the 'Charming Squire'. I explained to him once that the name matched Thomas perfectly, that he was my charming squire. We would listen to the music in the pub as he watched me try to build a house of cards with the cardboard coasters. Thomas encouraged my triumphs but enjoyed my crashing failures even more. Little boys and their love of tumbling constructions. We had a table that was always free and we'd sit together while I had something to eat and he would play games or watch his favourite shows on the iPad.

Other days we would head for what Tom called the Chinese Temple. Not far from the Queensland Performing Arts Centre is a boardwalk that meanders through a man-made rainforest and over a running creek of small waterfalls. At the end, the path opens up to a paved square surrounded by a thick wall of towering bamboo. Our first time there we investigated the inside of the 'Temple'. Quite a small interior but Tom could reach out and feel the carved walls and be amazed by something that was from far away. I discovered much later, after all of our Southbank walks were well past, the structure is actually a Nepalese Peace Pagoda. But Tom called it the Chinese Temple which was fine with me. We would sit and watch the fountains bubble and the tourists wander through the square. Then we would start our journey back to Lady Cilento. Our home, our work, our life.

On our walk back to the hospital, just before the traffic lights is a small hill. I would have to work hard to keep hold of Tom going down the hill but the push up at the end of a long walk was quite the challenge. There is a water bubbler not far from the start of the Goodwill Bridge and at the base of this small hill. Whether we were coming back from Southbank or from across the bridge exploring the Botanical Gardens on the northern side of the river, this was the bubbler we would visit. As part of Tom's therapy, he was encouraged to do as much reaching, pushing, pulling – anything to improve his strength and core balance. He would reach out and push down the handle for the water to flow. I would bend down and drink. It was another favourite ritual of ours. He was able to do something for me, just like he would press the buttons at the traffic lights and in the elevators up and down the hospital floors. The water bubbler was all about preparation for the hill though. We had to top Mummy up before she attempted her daily task of getting us up the hill. I'd say, "Ok Tom, here it is. I need your help, let's get up there. We're a team, spur me on". All the way up as I pushed my boy in his wheelchair, Tom would yell "Go Mum! You can do it Mum, my mum rocks, go Mum!" We were a team. He was my team.

I well remember those traffic lights at the top of the hill. A busy hub of traffic through South Brisbane, close to the city, a couple of private high schools and the hospital precinct of Lady Cilento and the Mater Hospital. We would be amongst a diverse crowd of hospital staff, tourists, students, commuters and families. When first starting our walks, I learned to be very prepared. We headed off on a walk one day after a particularly difficult night. He'd been up all night vomiting and I had been up all night cleaning. Most walks we didn't need a vomit bag – it was just for emergencies. The really vital addition to our walk was a good pile of napkins, or spit towels as we called them. However, this morning, it seemed we did need that vomit bag and it was at these lights at the start of our trip that Tom brought forth the contents of his tummy. It was quite an impressive spew that thankfully did not catch any nearby pedestrians. All I had were my napkins and his towel that he liked to rest his feet on. Well, we did our best to clean up, then I wrapped my scarf around his front for some semblance of dignity and we made a quick return back to the ward for a shower. After that, the pack list for a walk always included spit towels and a vomit bag!

So, we had our therapy and we had our walks but there were times we were not able to leave the ward. Tom's high occurrence of infection meant many courses of intravenous antibiotics during our time in hospital. Overcoming the boredom was a challenge – particularly at first when Tom's abilities were still in the early stages. We broke up our days with time completing puzzles, reading, watching TV and playing fine motor games on the iPad. The Allied Health therapists had such a great collection and so I would watch and promptly download Tom's favourites after our sessions. His favourites were from the 'TOCA Education' collection – a bundle of different games. A lot of 'drag and drop' apps with creative outcomes compared to timed challenges which were stressful and upsetting if he couldn't keep up. Tom's artistic side flourished with these and he could spend hours creating new meals in the kitchen, costumes, tattoo stylings and 'hairdos' for every different character. He explored virtual cartoon hospitals, vacation settings and haunted houses.

A NEW HOME

These were our days; some boring, some full of fun and adventure, some complicated by tests, scans, medication and infections. As Thomas was often at high risk of, or enduring constant infections, we were always in a private room which was a small mercy. We could keep our little world as we wanted it. When Tom was being treated for an infection, the doctors would put us on 'droplet control' and as a result, all nurses, therapists and doctors had to don gowns and masks that were binned as soon as they left the room. Our nights in hospital were far different to those at home. Thomas had always been a good sleeper. The thumb would go in his mouth and he wouldn't move too much until the new day. After months in hospital he learned to sleep through the constant interruptions of nurses taking observations and beeping machines. Thomas would wake for spits, vomits and nappy changes. He'd wake in pain with a burning in his throat and gut that doctors couldn't explain away or fix. I'd write it all down because I knew I'd be so tired after a big night that I might forget my questions for the doctors.

My priorities around meeting with doctors changed gradually over our time living on the wards. Once upon a time it was important that I be showered and dressed, hair and face done, ready for the ward rounds to chat with these professionals who called on us once or twice a day. After a long night up with Tom, one morning I wasn't ready – I was still in my pyjamas on a fresh cup of instant coffee when our team arrived at the door and I thought – well here we are. Dr Steve would sometimes come around quite late. The end of the day for him but we'd already be back in our pyjamas. He'd catch me smashing some Uber Eats and the free chocolate milk from the parent kitchen. We'd make some plans and chat about Thomas. Nobody else was too worried about my messy hair and pyjamas and so neither was I. All the doctor visits went the same way. I gave my report of how we were since they had last seen him. I'd give the count of vomits, poos, wees, pain complaints, calorie intake from the pump. I would check my notebook for new information or questions. Doctors would come over to check Tom out. He would sometimes engage with them, sometimes not.

So, here we were in this new home, with a new community of people in our lives. This home taught us patience and we got creative with how to spend our time. I watched Thomas charm the nurses. What amazing people these nurses are. The dignity they gave Tom regardless of what physical dilemma we were in when the call button went off. The patient, empathetic and always cheerful conversations they would have with him. With me. Thomas had months of 'numbers' and at times would be adamant that he didn't want a bar of it. He didn't want his arm squeezed by the cuff, light shone in his eyes or probes clipped on to his fingers. Tom's eyebrows would come down and his wrath would be clear. I would insist Tom be kind and let the staff do their job. Without a hint of irritation these men and women would assure Tom that it wasn't fair he had to deal with this stuff, that they understood and that they were sorry. They'd push through gathering data and all the way, compliment his bravery, his strong muscles and his sweet nature.

I can't say strongly enough that the nurses that cared for Tom were so incredible. A few instances left a bad taste in my mouth and at times I did have to advocate for Thomas, but generally, over the time at Lady Cilento Children's Hospital Tom was given such wonderful care. I remember some beautiful experiences that made all the difference. There was a time we had just changed wards, almost in the middle of the night. He slept through the move and I chatted to our new nurse on the way to our new accommodations. Thomas had just had his last dose of curative chemotherapy that day and was well and truly smashed. On hearing about the milestone, this very sweet nurse insisted that we celebrate Tom's achievement. She acknowledged the hard road he had been on. Then she made him a special card and brought in the last few toys from the prize box that a seven-year old boy would enjoy.

I recall a lovely girl from 8A who was smitten with Thomas. She always wanted cuddles and visited Tom even when she wasn't assigned his room. We would find notes for him when we arrived

A NEW HOME

back from a walk to say she missed him and lay on the praise for each of his new milestones. Thomas loved grabbing at the staff identification cards and swipe key cards hanging off the doctors and therapists. These were on a tether attached to their clothing and he would challenge himself to get a hold of them and pull. I can't remember if it was a nurse or another staff member, but one woman took the time to make Tom his own swipe/ID card on a tether clip. We attached it to his wheelchair so he could swipe us in and out of the wards and the main hospital doors each day. Such a simple thing but it made him feel so special.

Then there were the nurses that looked after me. I remember after a long period without a bowel movement from my boy, one particular nurse helped me clean up the absolute disaster area that followed. I was so grateful to have someone's help and he was so kind about it. Another day, after an especially difficult day with Tom in the Close Obs room, a nurse popped her head in that night and caught me crying. She sat down next to me and after a minute, she told me I was an amazing mum and tomorrow was going to be better. As my closest friend from school, Danielle, is a nurse practitioner she was always ready to listen, to advise, to help me understand the 'medical' stuff that was sometimes confusing and confronting. So, I send a big thank you out to those who cared for us in hospital, who go the extra mile, even when they are falling asleep on their feet, but we would never know – you make such a difference.

Practical Advice:

- Uber Eats is always an option.

- Have some extra bags in the room for surprise room changes – particularly for the toys.

- If you can get out for a walk remember to pack: your phone, spit towels, a towel for the foot stands, a vomit bag and blankets in case it got cold or if you want to have lie down on the grass. I also left a note with our return time in case we came back to a new nursing shift.

- If people offer to 'gift' you food, ask for it in single serve sizes. A lasagne for 6 doesn't fit so well in a hospital fridge.

- Hospitals can be so boring for kids (even for adults). Get creative, ask the allied health team for advice, where possible get a change of scenery.

- Love the flavoured milk but remember to drink water too.

- Nurses are there to help and can be your best allies but don't forget you are the one to advocate for your child if you are worried about anything.

- <u>Supporters:</u> I really appreciated food delivery vouchers (e.g. Uber Eats) and it was nice to have organised visits from *well* people. Don't bring flowers – gifts to kill the boredom are better.

- <u>Co-parents (but also everyone):</u> Keep a notebook for the 'counts', questions and milestones. It helps for handover and keeps track of things for each parent over time.

Chapter 4

Ringing the Bells

Watching Treatment ...

Radiation and Chemotherapy

Life in the hospital was one thing but the actual business end of the hospital was another. Cancer treatment was big and scary for someone like me who had only a basic grasp of what was to come. Thomas didn't know the extent of what was to come for him. Before Tom began treatment, his tumour needed to be categorised into one of the four subgroups. There are currently four groups: WNT, SHH and Groups 3 and 4. Thomas' tumour was classified in 'Stratum N1' under the St Jude assessment criteria which was under the Group 3 or 4 category. We were told that there was a good possibility of recovery, or remission because we had some great outcomes in our corner:

    a) The surgeons had achieved full resection – the tumour was out,

b) There had been no metastasises upon diagnosis – it had not spread beyond the initial tumour and,
c) The cancer cells of his tumour post-surgery did not look aggressive under the microscope.

This was all good news.

A lot of the research into medulloblastoma is currently focused on tailoring treatment to best suit the patient considering their subgroup. St Jude Children's Research Hospital in Memphis is the base for the main international trial in this research called **SJMB12**. Dr Steve told me a beautiful story about this hospital. Danny Thomas, a struggling comedian in the 1950's was broke. He promised St Jude, the patron saint of lost causes, that if he made it big he would make a shrine to him. Danny Thomas became extremely successful and used his wealth to fund the St Jude Children's Research Hospital. *Danny* was the name my Aunt Meg used to call my Dad. *Thomas* was the name I gave to my son. A beautiful little coincidence in a story of faith and generosity. A shame though that I had to hear of this lovely tale amidst the harsh realities of my son's brain cancer.

The trial known as **SJMB12** is continuous and corroborates data rather than testing hypotheses. They use historical data from cases all over the world to find the best standard for treatment decisions. A tricky balancing act to ensure sufficient impact on the cancer whilst keeping the toxicity at a minimum for the children. Tom's protocol of treatment was decided according to his subgroup which listed 30 rounds of radiation therapy and four cycles of chemotherapy.

During the six-week block after Tom's resection procedure, I was visited by a doctor from the radiotherapy department. She explained that Tom would need radiation therapy aimed at his whole brain and spine as well as weeks of focused blasts at the site of the tumour. In order for this to happen, Tom needed to be completely still. They would make a frame of his head and chest and apply stickers to his chest and belly to line him up each day. The planning process was so important – he needed to be in the exact position each time. Tom was unable to be still when conscious regardless of how hard he might have tried. This meant that each day, five days a week, Thomas would undergo a general anaesthetic before his radiation treatment.

Undergoing general anaesthesia every day was exhausting. It was like prepping for surgery every morning. Consent discussions with the anaesthetist and constant 'obs' from delivery and recovery nurses. Between late January and March, Tom's weekday routine was night-time fasting, morning pick up heading to radiation and then he'd return – usually fast asleep. The nurses in recovery learned early on that Tom would take hours to come out of his anaesthetic and so would send him up before he regained full consciousness most of the time. One little stir and they would send him on his way so he could go back to sleep. I remember those walks with the wards men/women and the nurse, to and from the radiation building. We went to great lengths attempting to mitigate the brightness and noise – the effect of posterior fossa was still a big deal for Tom and lying down on the bed facing the ceiling, he constantly had the lights in his eyes.

The hospital and the radiation clinic were adjacent and internally connected by an open-air corridor. This was my least favourite part of the trip. This outdoor pathway was plain concrete, quite dirty with spiderwebs along the walls and subject to weather. We walked through wind and rain but usually extremely bright sun which highly impacted Tom lying on the bed. I'd try to build a tent with pillows and blankets so he wouldn't notice our transition to the outdoors and so his sensitivity to light and noise was minimised.

I called it Prison Camp Corridor. This stretch of our walk somehow symbolised to me the horror of what Tom was facing. I was walking him to a treatment that was never meant to be for him. Tom didn't ask for it, didn't deserve it, but was trapped by it. I knew it would impact his body, have him vomiting in the afternoon after a long time recovering from the anaesthetic. Each visit would bring us closer to the loss of his hair. I knew this and eventually Tom came to know this. It was hurting him to help him, to save him. I was the warden walking with her young prisoner, but also a mum trying to save his life. I felt pulled in two directions and the paradox of my guilt and purpose was profound.

The connecting walkway between the hospital and the Radiation building

The doctor from the Radiation Department also explained to me what to expect in terms of side effects. The short-term side effects of radiation and daily anaesthetic were one thing to consider: nausea, vomiting, headaches, fatigue and of course losing his hair. I remember seeing the pillows collect more hair each day. Poor Tom would turn his face and his cheeks, sometimes wet with spit, would get covered in hair. He became so uncomfortable and so it had to go. I was worried he would be upset about it. He still wasn't talking so I didn't know if this was a big deal for him, but my fears were unfounded. Tom was never too worried about his appearance and he was far happier with clear pillowcases after that day. The blade one haircut slowly morphed into a perfectly bald head. Tom's gorgeous head absolutely rocked the bald look and over time I barely remembered him with a full head of hair.

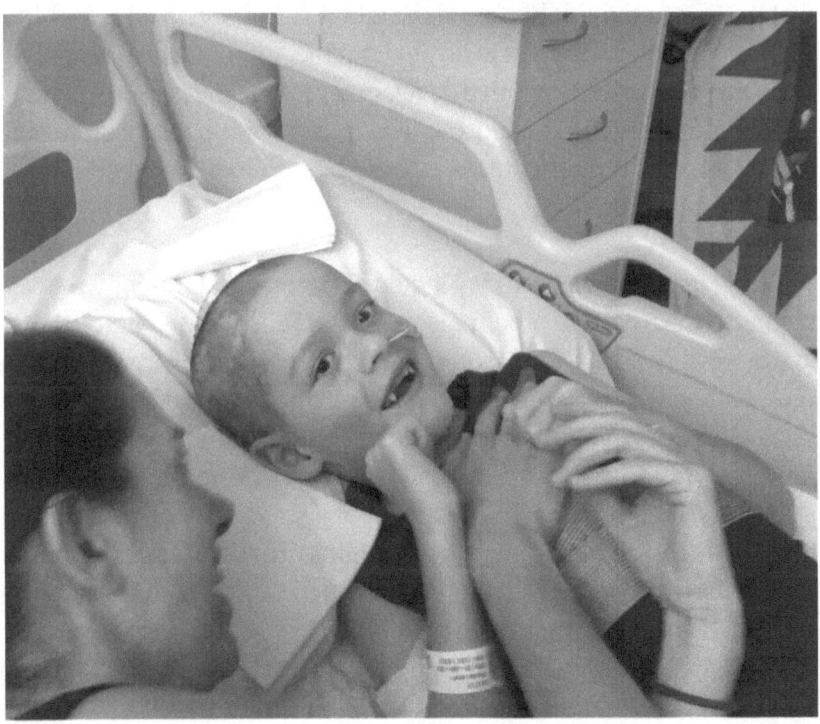

In children, apparently the likelihood of long-term side effects of radiation therapy is far increased as their nervous system is still developing. The pituitary would be impacted which is why paediatric protocols really only incorporate brain and spine radiation in children older than three. We were told to expect a possibility of stunted growth. Not really a big deal, but it would be a point of difference between the two boys. There was a high chance that Tom could end up infertile. I thought, well at least he has a twin with identical DNA, so there are options to alleviate that if it were an issue one day. I remember the doctor telling me that from now on Thomas would be at a higher risk of other cancers. That his lifestyle would need to be carefully considered in terms of drinking, smoking, sun safety, diet, etc. Already, I had confronted the idea that Tom would never be able to drink alcohol. Even the simple symptoms of a hangover such as lethargy, a headache, balance issues, etc would resemble the symptoms of an issue with his shunt. I was already playing out conversations where I would explain that the things some of his friends would do were not possible for him. Even though it was 10 years away it was more for him to deal with. The list went on: possible cognitive developmental effects, possible hearing loss, possible organ damage, etc. The cure would be as detrimental as the disease I thought but even these possibilities were better than him not surviving.

Walking to radiation each day led us on a path past the canvases on Level 2. There was no other reason for me to see these photographs apart from heading to prison camp corridor. Each canvas caught the image of happily recovered children; back home, back to their lives. Sunshine, colour, smiles, green grass, toys, surrounded by family. One canvas was different. It was a close-up photograph of a child's cremation urn. In the shape of a small, smoothly metallic bird with the name Sophie on it. I hated that canvas. I hated to see it, but my eyes were drawn to it every time. The innocence of this little bird and the tragedy amplified by its placement next to the images of surviving children. Every day it caught my eye and I came to be staring it down, determined that this canvas would not be our outcome. It would not happen to us.

RINGING THE BELLS

One day I saw a magnet left in a room we were moved into after our chemotherapy meds had finished up. It was for the contact details of the Palliative Care Team. I hurled it at the bin, and it had me close to tears for the next hour. Even though along the way we were assured Tom's chances were really good for recovery and remission. Even though I should have felt comfortable in the prognosis and the treatment we were receiving, in the back of my mind perhaps I knew that at any time, the next MRI, the next headache, the next small room conversation might lead to my fridge hosting that magnet or Tom's name on that urn. That possibility had me enraged. I was resolute it would not be us.

Tom spent more time in hospital than most kids on chemotherapy. As a result of his brain injury, the doctors negotiated a four-week block of rehabilitation as an inpatient. This took place between radiation and his first chemotherapy cycle. Tom's doctors tried to ensure Tom had at least one week at home before starting each cycle. This wasn't going home to stay – these were visits home, but we always had a return date. His protocol only meant for three or four days of chemo with a top-up on Day 8, but Tom was usually in for weeks following his treatment. His *neutropenia* (see Appendix 1 for further detail) meant that he was constantly fighting infections and hooked up to IV antibiotics. The side effects of the chemo were far reaching with Thomas. The level of toxicity in him was high and his body struggled to combat this. His rate of infection also saw him visit the Paediatric Intensive Care Unit on more than one occasion. Tom was on the standard cocktail of chemotherapy drugs for his type of tumour: Vincristine, Cisplatin and Cyclophosphamide. The doctors gave him two other medications to counteract the impact of the chemotherapy in terms of protecting organs and function. These were Amofostine and Mesna, and were accompanied by copious anti-nausea and anti-vomiting medication. Tom also underwent multiple blood transfusions and transfusions of platelets each cycle to boost his recovery (see Appendix 1 for more information on the side effects of medulloblastoma chemotherapy).

As much as the doctors tried to stem Tom's constant vomiting, we never really had any decent reprieve. For over nine months I would say the longest Thomas would go without vomiting would be for a few days. Most days after treatment could mean multiple vomits. I personally detest the feeling of nausea and the action of vomiting – I avoid it at all costs and so it was so difficult to watch the hundreds of vomits that Tom would endure during his treatment. I can't imagine how hard it was for him, particularly at the start. After a time living in the Rehabilitation Ward (8A) during his radiation treatment, Tom's vomiting started to instil fear in me. It was not for the fact that he would lose more calories and not for the clean-up. Rather, it was for the possibility of him throwing up his nasogastric tube. If it came up, it had to go back in. It is a terrible thing to have to restrain your child while a tube is pushed down his throat. Telling him to be calm, to swallow even though he can't. Telling him that screaming, crying and thrashing will only make it more difficult, that it's not a punishment but he has to endure it. Without this tube, he would not receive his medicines and he would slowly starve. Again, the lesser of two evils and so there we were, time after time – pushing that tube back up his nose and down into his stomach. Removing tape and reapplying it while he cried and pleaded with us to stop.

I was never a sickly child but when I remember being sick, I would think of how my mum would look after me. She'd stroke my forehead if I had a headache, keep me clean and fresh with new sheets when I got the sweats, clean up any vomit with a world of patience and praise for how well I was doing. I never felt in trouble or upset about making a mess because my mum would say "Good girl Trishy-Trocks". She'd say that anything can be cleaned up, that I'd be fresh as a daisy and feeling better soon. I would see her kind face and watch her fuss around and then she would give me time to sleep. She had three other kids, an over-worked husband, and my two grandmothers to care for as well but she could always make me feel better. She made us all feel better. I'm so thankful for my beautiful mum for what she taught me. I channelled her time and again when I was with Tom and it made everything easier to know how much impact my care would have had on him. That I could be his solid ground in a sea of pain and discomfort. This was my hope.

After months of dealing with this consistent routine of throwing up, Tom started to somewhat adapt to it. He mostly knew when it was coming, and we got very good at 'playing catch'. We'd have those handy bags at the ready and some vomits would be over pretty quickly. He became so accustomed to the repetitive nature of it all he happily coined a new name for himself: "Thomas the Vomits". He was pretty proud of himself with that one and many a nurse got to hear about it. We felt we were a team when confronted with each new spew – he'd make the call, I'd grab the bag and towel, he'd let me know when it was finished, and I'd clean up as needed. I couldn't believe something so ragged and vile could become almost procedural. Tom was an absolute champion about it all. I remember when he would let me know of the imminence of a spew, my head would say: 'No, baby, don't throw up again, surely not again. Please don't, please!' I would wish it away, but it always came.

My favourite story of Tom and his many vomits was one I posted to my community on Facebook. I wanted to share with everyone how amazing my boy could be.

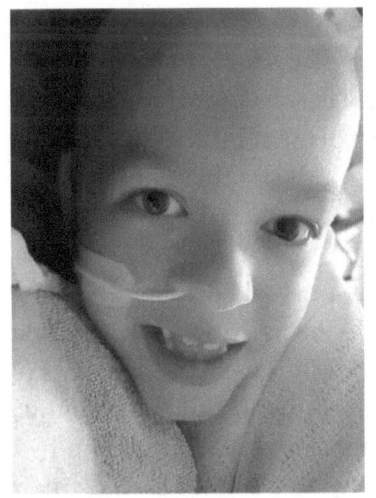

Trish Carpenter
20 Apr. 2018 at 2:57 am

The story behind this new profile pic..
It's 2:20am and Tom's just suffered through a hideous vomit. I scoop him up in a fresh blanket to get us out of the way while the nurses work to clean up and sort out fresh sheets. I look down at this delicious face and I say to him "aww Tom what a beautiful smile". He replies "I'm smiling because I know it makes you happy. I love you Mum." I reply "I love you right back bub - thanks for that sunshine in the middle of the night". 😢😊😌😌

Lindy Morgan and 111 others   19 Comments

👍 Like   💬 Comment   ➢ Share

I'll never forget how thoughtful Thomas was that night and always. How he tried to take care of me. I loved how we would find ways to make it ok, even though it wasn't. Another time he was sitting up in his wheelchair and we were drawing one afternoon. He said to me clearly and carefully, working hard to speak each syllable:

"You get another reward."

"What do I get a reward for?" I replied.

"For caring for me, and this time you get four," he said while holding up four fingers.

"Four rewards for caring for you?" I repeated.

"Yep," he nodded.

"Oh sweetpea. I'm a lucky lady."

"Yes," he said.

"I love you."

I had been recording his drawing efforts right before this conversation and so I captured this 'reward chat' too. I watch it still. Anytime guilt comes to call and I despair that I didn't do enough. This short video of my smiley boy reminds me that perhaps I did enough for him. That I did all I could do.

Each cycle of chemotherapy would get pushed back by infections and slow recovery of blood counts. Eventually, the fourth cycle was complete. The MRI following the final cycle was clear. We had made it to the end of oncology treatment! So many vomits, temperatures, therapy milestones, smiles and tears and Tom had made it to the end. When kids move up to a higher level in their swimming lessons, they get to ring the bell to acknowledge their achievement. Before entering the world of oncology this was my only experience of a bell ringing ritual. It's also an oncology tradition to celebrate the end of a patient's treatment by ringing a bell. On Tom's last day of radiation, a small group of us assembled in the waiting room. Some nurses, Owen, myself and Tom. He still wasn't talking or able to sit up very well at this point, but he had control of movement. Tom loved the blankets I would bring from home – they were colourful and super soft for snuggling. My bright blue blanket lay across the white sheets and we manoeuvred the tilt and height of the bed so he could reach. With a beautiful smile on his face as he concentrated on his task, Tom rang the bell. We clapped, we cheered, and he smiled. It was a happy day.

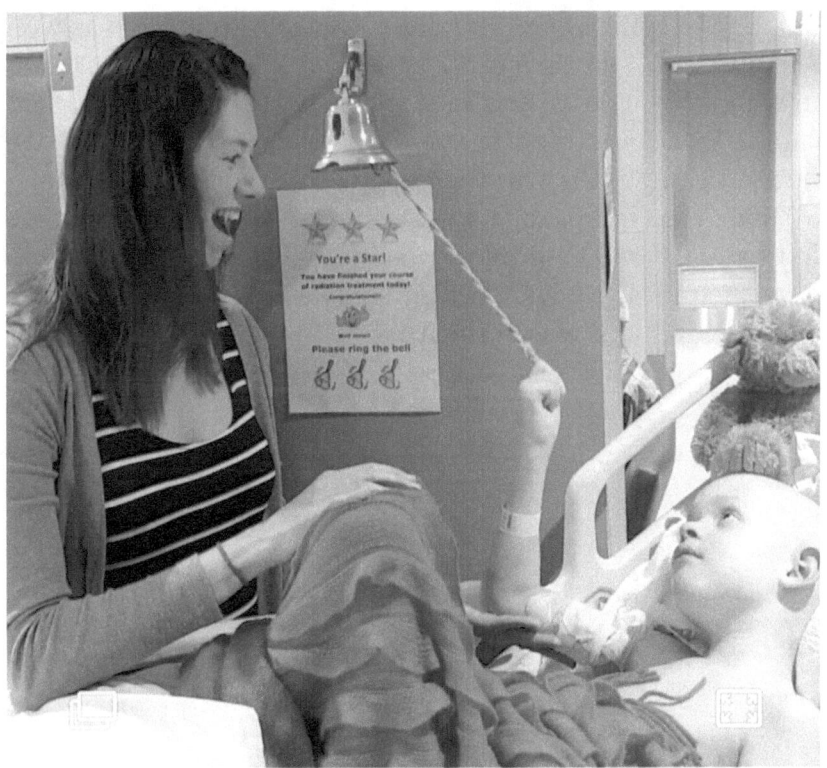

Radiation Bell-Ringing – 2nd March 2018

BIG HAND, LITTLE HAND

The bell signalling the end of chemotherapy was to be a far more notable affair. Almost five months after the start of his chemotherapy treatment and three beautifully clear MRI scans - we were ready to celebrate! Surrounded by family and Tom's wonderful team of doctors, nurses and therapists, I moved Thomas over to the board and the golden bell. He rang the bell in the sunshine, signed the board, received his certificate and enjoyed the applause and congratulations. I loved watching him smile and laugh. He had been through so much and it was over. I was so proud of this little boy ringing a bell in the middle of the fifth floor garden. The feeling of relief and pride we all felt for Tom was just magical. Cam stood beside him and Tom smiled as everyone there showed him their appreciation, told him how amazing he was, how hard he had fought. A moment in time where his battle against his cancer was won and he would start to feel better. He would be free to get right into his rehabilitation and back to himself before this wretched cancer had taken the lifestyle he'd known. This is what we knew then and this was the hope for the future. After many a photo, the staff headed back to their busy workday and we left Lady Cilento Children's Hospital with a sense of joy that I can't express. We went for milkshakes and a chicken lunch afterwards and it was beautiful.

RINGING THE BELLS

Oncology Bell-Ringing – 14th September 2018
Thomas surrounded by his medical and therapist team

There's a song that takes me back to the more difficult times with my little boy in hospital called **"Orpheus"**. This song wasn't released while Thomas was undergoing treatment, but when I first heard it, I was reminded of our long nights together. Our battle year of 2018. Thomas wasn't as scared and agitated as the first few weeks. He slept a lot in the weeks of radiation, coming out of his daily general anaesthetic by lunchtime, going for a walk and then back for night-time. We started chemotherapy in March/April. These months of treatment for Tom meant he was sick and tired and hurting. Settled amidst the chaos of his vomits, his spits, soaring temperatures, scans, lumbar punctures, blood tests, transfusions and his boredom when trapped on the IV. It was a time that hurt my heart again and again.

BIG HAND, LITTLE HAND

This song personifies the mood of our time in 11B - Oncology Ward. When we would listen to music together, handle things when he was sick and just muddle through until we could get out for a walk. Sometimes I think I was more broken by this time than Tom. He was usually pretty happy to play on the iPad, working on puzzles or elbow-deep in Lego. Kids are so amazing at how well they deal with all of this, but I was tired, heartbroken and trying to keep up the façade. Chanting each time, "it'll be alright darling, we'll talk to the doctors again tomorrow about fixing this, never mind sweet pea". It's hard to comfort your baby and promise that things will get better when you know there is still a long road of suffering ahead. That there are no guarantees and that while it is all very necessary, it was you who signed him up for this pain. Then the guilt comes calling again, and so you pretend that you believe those words: "It's going to be okay". Otherwise how can you smile, how can you look him in the eye and ask him to be brave one more time? And then another time and another.

The song resonates with me as a conversation I am having with Thomas. When I look back on our time in hospital – the hard times but also the good, this song is from the perspective of us having one of our chats, snuggled up in bed. The poetry of each lyric describes my hopes of helping him get through the chaos of his treatment and comforting him the only way I know how.

Practical Advice:

- Take breaks, alternate with your spouse, your family. Find ways to get sleep if every night is routinely hectic.

- Remember what comforted you when you were a sick kid.

- It's hard on you but it's harder on them so do your best to be patient – this is particularly tricky when you are sleep-deprived and an emotional wreck.

- Get comfortable with washing your hands, wearing masks, saying no to visitors who have small kids or any sickness.

- Try to build a routine but don't get too upset if it doesn't happen – there are good days and bad days.

- Climb in to have a cuddle as often as they want you to.

- Take photos and videos of progress and chats if you get a chance.

- Ask for help with clean up, particularly if it's a big one. They are no fun to do solo. Your focus is your bub. It also means the nurses know to add it to the chart if needed.

- <u>Supporters:</u> Give blood and plasma. Stay away if you are sick!

- <u>Co-parents:</u> The logbook is crucial when dealing with this stuff so you know things like:

    - if it's been a hard night

    - if your child will be bone tired

    - if something worked well

    - if something new presented

    - if there was any nutrition happening and approx. how many calories got through

    - what to tell the doctors if you handled the hard stuff all by yourself and it might not have been charted.

Chapter 5

High Hopes

Rehabilitation

This might seem ridiculous but initially I didn't want to take Tom home. When Tom started chemotherapy in April 2018, we had been living in hospital for four or five months. My boy was unable to ride in the car, we had no comfortable bathroom commode for showers and toileting, and I wasn't confident I could look after him without nurses at the ready. I thought if we could stay in hospital, he'd get more rehab work with his therapists than the few offered by the 'Physio in the home' program and we could continue our little routines of walks, visitors, school and the rest of it.

So we took it slowly; a day visit here, a weekend there until we got a week at home between each cycle. Start days of chemotherapy cycles were often pushed back for Tom, particularly in the later months. Each time it took his body longer to recover in terms of platelets, haemoglobin, antibiotic courses and overall wellness.

For short visits we were able to make do and it gave us an idea of what preparation we needed to do for the long term. We learnt that our bathroom needed a complete overhaul to accommodate a commode both in the shower and access to the toilet. Some of the most amazing people came together to bring about a full bathroom renovation in a matter of weeks. We fashioned a feed pump stand out of a hat stand and built or found small portable ramps to smooth out the bumps to the back patio.

I remember the day we packed up our room to go home for the long haul. It seemed to be a much bigger deal for me than Tom. He was so used to just going with the flow – perhaps he didn't understand the enormity of it. We had no booking date to return. Yes, we had outpatient visits, rehabilitation work and if infection struck again…we would be back, but technically we had finished treatment. The last MRI was clear as a bell and so we could turn our focus to Tom's brain injury. We could move back home, start a new routine and have our family back together. It was exciting!

It was September, and the school term was moving towards holidays. We had meetings booked with the Queensland Paediatric Rehabilitation Service to discuss a new plan. Once we had finished up with oncology, we said goodbye to our Allied Health team and signed up with a new one as outpatients. We were given a finite block of rehab time – eight weeks. After this time Tom would move to community providers with the National Disability Insurance Scheme. This service was still new, so we had already started the application for assistance. For now though, we were home together, and we had a plan.

With our return home, I had entered a new role. I had already taken on the job of physiotherapist, occupational therapist and nutritionist but the role of nurse was one I took very seriously. The nurses had watched me prepare Tom's meds many times while on the ward but at home, there were no reminders, no advice, no charts. I had my pharmacy list with dose instructions and times that I came to memorise. Tom was on such a mix of things at all different times: gabapentin, potassium, voriconazole, omeprazole, anti-nausea meds, pain meds and sometimes laxatives too. Mostly meds were morning, lunch and afternoon but at times I was up giving a 2am med for one or two weeks at a time. I was partly thankful for his nasogastric tube – it meant that I wasn't waking him or forcing him to swallow each one. All of Tom's medications had to go down his tube which meant getting them into a syringe. The pill crusher tool that I had wasn't really a help as some of the tablets were so small that I could barely get the powder out of it. So for tablets, I did something else. I would get out a clean bread board and a small sharp knife. I'd cut the half section I needed and then I would press it with the knife as a first crush. Then I would chop it into the finest powder I could. I called it cutting the cocaine. I've never personally cut cocaine, but we've all seen the movies. It was a fun little pretence we had that I was super hard core. I would say to Owen: "Where's my cutting board? I gotta cut me some cocaine!"

The new routine for our day-to-day life was simple. We'd all pile in the car each morning. First stop was to Cameron's school and then Tom and I would make the journey into Lady Cilento Children's Hospital. Level 6 was our new assignment and each week we were given our schedule. Different combinations and time slots but usually we would see our new speech therapist, physiotherapist, occupational therapist and also spend some time down at the Hospital School. Then we'd head back to the carpark and bundle ourselves back in for Cam's school pick up. We'd spend about 40 minutes in the car each way and I adored those trips. Thomas had developed the strength to sit up in a boosted car seat and while we'd listen to his songs he would dance and lip-sync. Tom had a great playlist of fun up-beat songs mostly from movies he liked or the radio. We would alternate songs from each other's playlists and dance all the way to and from the hospital. Two songs that really captured his attention and also become some of my favourites were **"Hair Up"** and **"High Hopes"**.

"Hair Up" is a song from the movie Trolls written over the music from Edvard Grieg's *Peer Gynt Suite I: In the Hall of the Mountain King*. While the vocal lines written for the purposes of the movie are more of a chant, I found the fact that Thomas loved this song so fitting considering what the original piece conveys. *In the Hall of the Mountain King* tells the story of the young protagonist – Peer Gynt – being chased by mountain trolls after offending their King. The music builds up in texture and increases in tempo, illustrating the chase and creating such an atmosphere of suspense. Peer Gynt must race faster and faster in order to escape, which he does but by the skin of his teeth. I often thought to myself how easily Tom sat in this metaphor – how he needed to work harder and harder in this time of rehabilitation. Racing in an effort to escape his trolls, his posterior fossa. Every day I saw him outrun them bit by bit.

For a time, Tom also loved the song **"High Hopes"** by Panic! At the Disco and it later became an absolute favourite of Cameron's as well. The lyrics are the perfect characterisation of our mindset during this rehabilitation block – mine and Tom's. 'High Hopes' set out our expectations and my belief in this courageous seven-year-old boy. The song speaks of a mother's advice, it talks about positivity, beating the odds and wanting 'everything'. Tom loved songs with energy and this song energised both of us every trip into the hospital and beyond.

So, we listened to the songs and we played car games. A favourite time-passer was our ongoing game of 'Spotto'. Spotto is a game where players try to be the first to see a yellow vehicle and yell SPOTTO! Points are tallied along the way and at the end of the journey, a winner declared. Thomas liked to allocate extra points for buses and trucks. He was the judge for the point scoring and whether or not a car had enough yellow on it to qualify. Tom was also the champion. Before his tumour, he was super quick and competitive. In 2018, I admit to allowing him the wins most of the time over the first few weeks in the car. His speed and concentration grew with each trip. I loved seeing his smiling face in the mirror when he would beat me to a call.

We would arrive at the carpark across the road from the hospital each morning. I had a set routine. The first step was to pull out the wheelchair and assemble it. I had definitely improved my upper body and core strength after the first few weeks of this and become quite the pro at setting it all up. Tom's main obstacle with coming home in the first place was his capacity to travel in a car. Maxi-taxi's which accommodated wheelchairs were too few and we would often be waiting for long periods of time. In between the chemotherapy cycles, our Allied Health Team made it a priority to work out appropriate arrangements for car seats and to train Tom and me in 'transfers'. I learned that transfers are a big deal for someone in a wheelchair. Tom had to be able to get from his chair into the car, onto the shower commode, onto the couch, onto the floor, into bed, the list goes on. Our wonderful physiotherapists Hayley and then Kate would say to me that every transfer is another act of rehab – more physiotherapy that is building his strength and his balance. So even when Tom was tired, I had to try to get him through a transfer. Even if it were easier for both of us for me to lift him here and there, we had to do the work.

To start with it was a matter of listing every little step he needed to take. Grab that bar, scoot your bum forward, push with your arms, hold on to me, turn and take a step…some we did well, others we struggled. If Tom was exhausted he would have less 'push' in him, but he would still follow the steps. If we were in a rush, we might not get our balance right. Most of the time though, he was brilliant. He listened and followed each instruction and over time it became second nature to him. I was always there to help him but each day, he needed me a little less for holding, catching, reminding, pushing. Car transfers were the most difficult manoeuvre and once he was in his seat, I would lean across him to buckle him in. Each time we had a super smooth and stress-free transfer I'd get nice and close, and I'd whisper, "Textbook!" I was so proud, and he would smile up at me. It became a little ritual for our best transfers – then he would say, "Mum …textbook!" before I got a chance.

One day when we arrived home from hospital, Cam climbed out and was heading to the back door. I was doing my thing – pulling out the wheelchair and all the bits to get it properly assembled. By this point, I was acting as more of a 'spotter' for Tom's exit transfers from the car. He knew the steps and could control his way out of the car. I came around from the back of the car with the wheelchair ready to go and found Tom standing outside the car. He was holding onto the interior of the door and the car seat with his other hand. His legs were straight, and his Batman Boots were firmly under him. I took it all in and the best part was the look on his face. Even though he'd broken the rule about waiting for me – he was absolutely glowing! Tom's face was a picture of pride and accomplishment. He had done it on his own. He remembered the steps; he executed the holds and moved his body the right amount and at the right angles.

I broke down and got on my knees to hug him while I cried and laughed and told him how incredible he was. I desperately hope the sight of him standing there and smiling at me that day stays in my memory for the rest of my life. What a perfect moment we shared. It was another time we had this feeling of teamwork, like we did when he would press the water fountain for me, encourage me to get us up the hill or to catch the next vomit. I was so proud to be on this team, with this amazing boy. Later, I took the time to say that he had to wait for me next time otherwise he might fall, that I knew he could do it himself but I just wanted to stand next to him in case of an accident or if his legs got too tired one day. But for that day, we were both flying high on this new achievement, this confidence.

So, back to our rehabilitation days, once in his chair, I would attach the feed pump, grab our bags, towels and blankets and we would set off for Level 6. Tom would press the elevator buttons, wave to drivers as we crossed the road and without fail, point to the gift shop as we entered the hospital. Tom's most intensive sessions were usually with his new physiotherapist Kate. As with Hayley, Tom's first physio, this woman was wonderfully patient and always looking for ways to creatively get Thomas working hard without him noticing. Hayley from the oncology team had introduced Tom to the hoist a little while back. We called it the Superman Hoist. Once strapped in, Tom would negotiate use of the control panel. Hayley would give him a goal and then he could have the remote. He would press that 'up' button until he was towering over us with

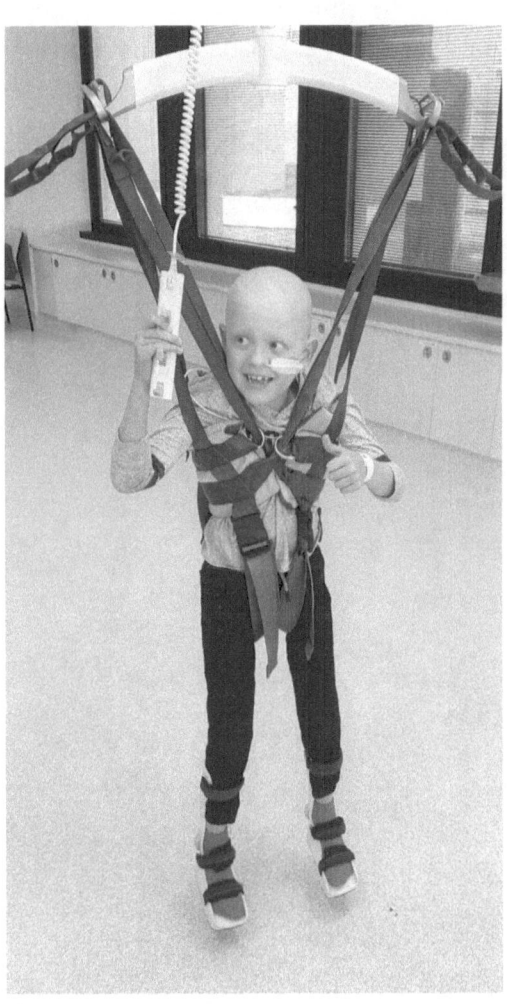

the biggest grin and squeals of delight. In the hoist, he practiced walking, turning, kicking balls and using walking aids. Kate had him try a leg press, lots of floor work and the bars but his favourite with Kate were the bikes.

While Thomas had never been a big bike-rider in the past, he felt a great sense of independence on the hospital bikes. Hesitant at first, as he was with every new piece of equipment, he came to love the three-wheelers. Strapped in and helmet on, we would go cruising through the corridors, out to the rehabilitation garden and activity area. He would play finding games along our path and chase me at speed. Sometimes other people walking along would offer to

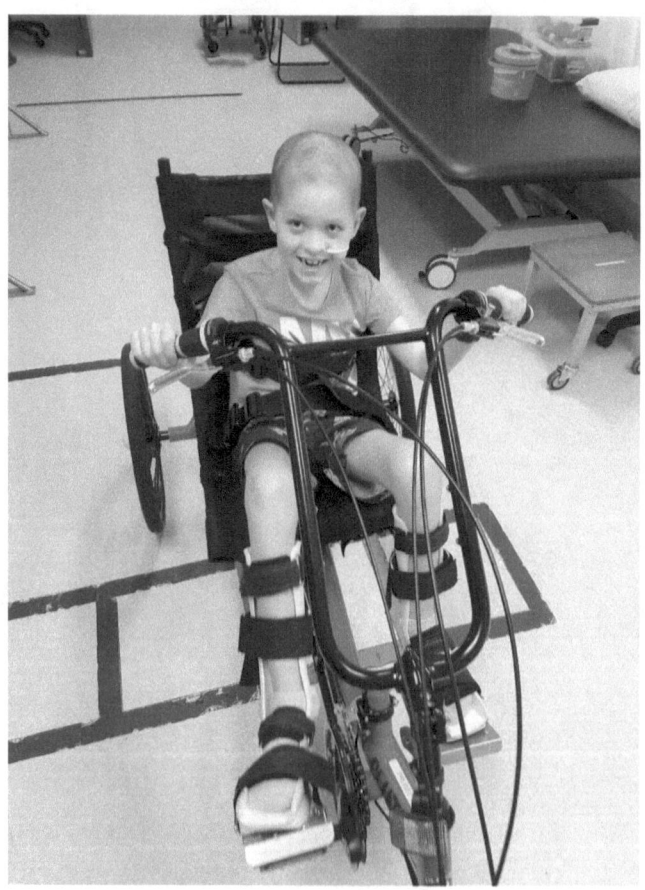

race and he'd get this intense face of effort and competition. We called it his 'Rocky' face. Sometimes we could go down and have a ride outside and one time, his brother Cameron was allowed to borrow one as well. It was another opportunity for him to feel like a kid again. To have some control: where he would go, how fast he would push. My face was on constant impressed mode with a healthy dash of verbal praise and pride at how fast and strong he was getting. There were times though that I was so overwhelmed it was all I could do not to cry. I remember the first time he stood up from a sit and the same day he pushed himself up onto all fours from lying face-down on the floor. First his arms and then his bum. I definitely cried that day I was so excited, so proud.

The other big favourite for Tom was Hydrotherapy: physio in the water. Once chemotherapy was completed, the doctors removed his central line and we were finally allowed to go swimming. With the assistance of his floaties and the physiotherapist, Tom enjoyed such freedom and the pool became a favourite activity for him. Tom's independence and what his body could manage in the water had him smiling and splashing and moving in every direction. It tired him out, but the pool visits were a constant request. Even on weekends – there would be a visit to a pool where he could swim with Cam, Owen and me. While he loved the water, Tom was never keen on showers. While he had a line in, either in his arm or chest, we had to bag it up before each shower and even more upsettingly take the cover off afterwards. It was a great day when the lines were gone but showers were still hard work. The occupational therapists were keen to have him practice washing himself and so I would give Tom the soapy washer and the shower hose. He would hate getting water in his eyes, so I would be at the ready with a hand towel to keep him onside with the ordeal. His only joy in the shower was trying to catch a pool of water in his lap and to hose me 'by accident'. The shower commode was a bit too high, was sticky when wet and not nearly as comfortable as his regular wheelchair. While it could often be a battle to convince Tom to have 'good grace' with the shower routine I absolutely loved that fresh smell of soap on him. I had loved it since I brought him home as a baby and it was no different now.

The occupational therapists in our new rehabilitation team were Sarah and Ali. Occupational therapy meant games and Thomas usually was willing to play with whatever they brought along. These games focused on his fine motor skills such as building, connection games (i.e. Lego) and proved very popular with Tom. He would get quite territorial about his creations though and insist no other kids could use the toys once he had made something. Without him realising, he was also working on his core and balance as these games would have to be played sitting on the floor, holding himself up, reaching across to get different pieces, etc. The day we tried him on the Wii Fit having a go at bowling as a joint session with physiotherapy, he was standing in his Ankle Foot Orthoses boots and a spotter stabilising his hips. Tom's frustration with the technique got the better of him but he was working so hard managing to stand, move, concentrate on a target and press the buttons at just the right time.

In speech therapy it was more games – those that had elements of questioning and identification. Nikki tried all sorts of things and his favourite was the microphone. He really enjoyed using his voice at different pitches to move things around in a computer program. The creativity of these therapists and all the tools that they have to work with kids amazed me. I loved seeing him enjoy the novelty of each new thing and work at improving and trying harder each time.

Most days, Thomas would get a chance to go to the hospital school. Tom enjoyed school during his rehabilitation far more than bedside visits from teachers. He liked the classroom environment even though he was the only one in a wheelchair. The other kids were so welcoming and made such a beautiful effort, more than you would see in a regular class. The teachers ensured he was offered every opportunity to learn. Before his tumour, Tom was always happy to play with others or alone. Having access to new toys, games, activities was great and became his focus during lunch breaks, but I think just being around other kids made a big difference to him. This was also the only session that parents didn't attend. The teachers were clear that they could manage without us and hovering parents didn't necessarily improve outcomes. So, we were sent on our way. This was another experience which brought Tom closer to normalcy – finally, a break from having a constant adult companion. A chance to talk with other kids, to work on stuff without mum or dad just around the corner. His handwriting was slowly improving but he preferred the iPad. Tom enjoyed story-time and even got to see things through a microscope one day. The teachers always had work to show at the end of a visit and positive things to report.

Tom's ability to swallow returned in August. We started with thickened fluids and Cheetos. This progressed bit by bit with new requests every day. Tom had been fixated on food for months and would often plan out our menu, which really meant he would decide what I would have to eat or drink. He had always been pretty good with food, willing to try new things and he had a real fondness for berries and cherry tomatoes. But on the return of his eating ability he enjoyed the savoury stuff – nachos became a constant favourite as did makeshift bacon burgers with cheese and tomato sauce. He loved his custard and once he was allowed to enjoy regular drinks Thomas was always keen for flavoured milk and those Up and Go Breakfast drinks. Most flavours were on the list, but lime was a favourite. I know, pretty hideous! Thomas wasn't eating enough food to be off the nasogastric tube and pump but how awesome was it to finally have new tastes to enjoy and the feel of food and drink in his mouth! Tom's swallow also began to mitigate the constant need to 'spit' and so we weren't running through tissues at a rate of knots anymore. It was an exciting time, but with the good comes the bad.

The first tricky obstacle we hit came after the third chemotherapy cycle. Tom had an audiology appointment after each round to check that no damage had occurred to his hearing. Before his last round of chemotherapy, Tom's audio tests came back with a deficit in his ability to hear high frequency sounds. The doctors adjusted his final chemotherapy medication and organised for him to be referred for hearing aids. Thomas never felt that he needed them and really, we only got them for when he would be in a classroom setting. Over time without them, there might have been a slight change in his ability to hear certain consonants and therefore this may have eventually affected his speech. So…we got them, and he chose superman blue. He never complained too much about them. I was always worried I'd forget he had them on and they'd get soaked in the shower or he'd take one out while lying down on the couch and we'd lose it.

The next development was a little more familiar. We always knew when Tom had had enough. Ever since he was little, his eyebrows were his most expressive feature and he was known for a fiery temper. Whether sad, happy or as a temper tantrum was about to take over, his eyebrows were in play. Throughout our days in rehabilitation, these angry eyebrows would come out. There were plenty of times when Thomas would just refuse with complaints of exhaustion. Sometimes these were even before we had started. Continued encouragement often resulted in the lowering of the eyebrows and a firm stance of rejection. For so long Thomas had gone with the flow, endured all that the doctors put before him. His strong will had never diminished but with returning home, he was back on his solid ground. His new routine was focused on getting his independence back, and with that came the return of the 'eyebrows'.

Thomas had also gradually become more serious in his temperament. At times he reminded me less of a little boy and more of a crotchety old man. Cam bore the brunt of Tom's new sensible attitude with reprimands coming from Tom's corner whenever his brother's behaviour got a bit silly. Thomas would even suggest punishments for Cam, which didn't go down well. Tom started using phrases like, "Seriously?" when asked to do things he felt were repetitive or ridiculous questions from therapists. My favourite was, "Oh, for Pete's sake!" There were times when I was a bit saddened by this early onset maturity that came as a by-product of his health battles. I preferred hearing him laugh and smile and act like a kid. This change was even more predominant considering his twin brother – when I could see such a difference between the two boys. The boys had always had their own personality and sensibilities, but they were so different to each other now.

I think Cam also felt such a difference in Tom, who once upon a time used to be so very mischievous, fun-loving and competitive. His brother was home again but now in a wheelchair and acting like…an adult. There was no more wrestling and chasing, no more backyard playtime and playground adventures. Cam would ask me, "When is Tom going to be back to normal?" He wanted his brother back – the brother that he remembered. I understood his frustration. I also wanted my Tom back as he once was, before the tumour, before the months in the hospital. I missed Tom's voice before his posterior fossa changed it. I missed watching the boys chase each other. I missed dancing with Tom in the kitchen after dinnertime. I missed the everyday life of my two healthy boys who went to school and played at the park on weekends. But that life was on hold – we had to be patient, hardworking and determined. Then we would find our way back there together and Tom would be stronger than ever.

So, we came up with new activities for the boys to do together. Lego was a keen favourite, as was painting, gardening, baking cupcakes, and our night-time tradition of 'readers' continued. Even though the boys would fight from time to time as they grew up, they learned to share early on. They shared a room, their toys, their clothes, their books and a daily routine. Now they were in separate rooms with different routines and different needs. I know that it was an adjustment for Cam to see the extra time I was spending with Tom. His transfers, his meds, his feed pump, his vomiting…the list went

on. To his credit, Cam started to join our team, particularly when it came to emergency stations surrounding a vomit or an urgent need for Tom to wee. Cameron was the fastest at getting the bottle or the vomit bags.

While we were off the ward, Thomas still went in for weekly checks as he was still on medication. The plan was for a slow weaning of meds but that meant blood tests and visits to the Oncology Day clinic on 5C. These appointments were such a trial, not so much seeing the doctors, but the waiting! We would sometimes wait for hours. This in itself was not just our problem – everyone in that waiting room had the same issue but my Thomas was the only one in a wheelchair. The only one who couldn't be bribed with yummy foods and active playtime in the kids' area. He was bored, at times exhausted and often he started to complain of a sore bum and back if the wait was too long. Sometimes he'd watch the entertainers who would come around but mostly, he just wanted to bury his head in the iPad. His favourite way to pass the time was to watch some Teen Titans or make new artistic creations on the Toca apps. Another option was watching funny YouTube clips about babies or kittens on my phone.

As far as we were told, Tom had just eight weeks of hospital rehabilitation time as an outpatient before we had to source therapy for him in the community. There had been delays with our National Disability Insurance Scheme application even though we had started the process months before. To get the most out of the time, we pushed Tom to really work hard. He was in back-to-back sessions and by the end of each day was exhausted. We knew it was hard work, but he had done the hard yards before when on the ward.

I didn't understand why his energy levels weren't better, why his vomiting was still an issue and as the weeks went past, we were still a fair distance from the ultimate goal of walking with an aid. We still had two weeks of therapy left in our block. This wasn't going to be enough time. The doctors couldn't explain it. Perhaps we didn't want to see that Tom's body wasn't coping? Far easier to suggest that it could be fixed with encouragement, asking for a positive attitude or chalking it up to a complication from his brain injury. None of these things were the answer, none of them was the problem. Our clue came with the headaches.

Practical Advice:

- Buy white towels. When home I missed the ever-full linen racks on the ward. I bought 10 white towels and was ready at home for every vomit, spit and clean up.

- For Tom's new wheelchair, we put in little diagonal risers or ramps to smooth ledges going to the bathroom and to the patio. Even on a ground floor house, these made life much nicer than jarring him each time or taking a run at a 'bump'.

- Keep a simplified list of meds all together on the kitchen bench if you have room.

- Build on and develop new rituals with your child. Things just between you and them. These bonded us together even more when the going got rough. Do the same for siblings so they can feel that they are special too in your eyes even though, your attention is sometimes prioritised differently.

- The perfect activity table: a trestle table is just the right height for a paediatric wheelchair (including armrests). Cover it with a thin piece of plywood. Cut a decent sized piece of green felt material to cover the ply. Voila! Lego pieces are easy to find on a block colour and pieces don't bounce away. Easy thing to lift away if half-way through a project and easy to shake off into a tub when finished. Also, it easily converts to a dinner table for the family afterwards.

- Apply for NDIS funding as early as you can. The allied health therapists will put together all of the reports for you. Get on to this quick – the application process alone can take a long time.

- <u>Supporters:</u> Take photos of the child and their parents, be sneaky if you need to. There should be more photos of parents with their kids, particularly when they are going through this together.

- <u>Co-parents:</u> Consider taking turns with attending therapy sessions. Experiment with how well your child responds with different combinations of people in the room. If 'all in' works best - great! If 'therapists only' gets better results, schedule in a few of these each week.

- <u>Co-parents again:</u> For physiotherapist appointments, invite your partners or support people in to watch and learn. Arrange different sessions for each side of the family to have time with your child and the physiotherapist to double check transfer techniques and to see your child's capacity in a therapy environment. If they are supporting you in your care – they should feel confident to do so.

Chapter 6

Another Small Room

Recurrence

November 2018. Thomas was working hard in rehabilitation but was still exhausted. He was eating a little but his main nutrition was through his nasogastric tube and the vomiting was still happening. Exhaustion and vomiting: these were signs and symptoms from the year before…but we didn't think it was a tumour. It couldn't possibly be a tumour. All of his MRIs had been clear since last December. Then, Tom had a series of terrible headaches and regular pain medication didn't help. We were due for our first follow-up MRI post treatment in December and were expecting a clear scan. These headaches were an alarm bell for me. I clung to the best possible reason which was that his shunt might have been failing. A failing shunt could be fixed, a simple procedure. We wouldn't know without an MRI though, so the scan was moved forward to November 13th.

Tom had managed to undergo his previous MRI without moving and so we tried him in the MRI without a full anaesthetic. He went in with the request of Smurfs II as his chosen movie. Tom didn't last the length of the scan. He called out, "Emergency! Emergency!" pressing his special button. The movie was too scary he said, he didn't want to go back in. I remember praying and repeating over and over, "it's just the shunt, it's just the shunt. They fail all the time – it must be the shunt". The scan was incomplete, but the doctors got a partial look. Tom had been sent back to the Emergency Room from Imaging where he settled down for a sleep. He hadn't slept well the night before and was fairly knackered.

Around dinner time, Dr Steve came down with a doctor from neurology. He didn't take us to a small room – instead it was a hushed conversation at the end of Tom's bed. The lights were off, the curtain closed, and Tom was snoring softly. The only other noise beside our whispers were the machines by Tom's bed. Dr Steve was serious; he had that face on when things aren't looking good – his 'small room' face. I'd seen it before, and I would see it again. He told me while they hadn't been able to see everything, they did find something. The tumour had returned. The egg was back. I said, "but couldn't it be the shunt?" The neurosurgeon assured me the shunt was working perfectly and my heart broke. We had so many questions, but Dr Steve kept saying until a complete scan could be reviewed, he couldn't answer them. We would know more tomorrow.

I had to get out. I left the room, walking to the waiting room. By the time I got out of the ward, I was running. I was crying. Not a tiny weep type of cry. A full blown ugly and loud cry that blinded me as I ran from the hospital. I ended up on the side of the road in the pickup zone on Level 1. I found a seat and bent over with my head in my hands. We were going to go through it all again. He was going to go back to square one, back through the phase of screaming, unable to talk or move. I thought to myself what terrible hell lay before us. A kind nurse had seen my dash from the building and came out to sit with me. She let me cry. She asked a few questions and tried to console me. She took my phone and called Owen and my friend Sharon who lived down the road. The nurse's name was Gabrielle and she sat with me until someone could take over. I remember saying to her, "Gabrielle is my middle name". A completely extraneous statement and irrelevant to the crisis I was in, but it popped into my mind and it came out of my mouth. Small talk mixed amongst the terror and pain of cancer. Funny the things you think and say when your world is crashing down around you.

I thanked her as another nurse arrived to sit with us and the rest of that next hour was a blur. My mind was racing with everything Thomas had been through and how we would manage to do it all again. Sharon arrived, then Owen. Standing in the pick-up zone of the Emergency Department I cried out every fear I had, an angry tirade of how unfair it all was. I held onto Owen with everything I had, and my legs buckled with each wave of realisation that Tom would have to be told. How would I tell him this? He'd been tortured before on the understanding that it was all over. That his good grace along the way would be rewarded with a clean bill of health and a path back to his old carefree life.

I needed to get my anger and my frustration out so I could take on tomorrow with a clean face and a positive outlook. We'd done it once; we could do it again. We would do it even better this time. Things would be easier the second time around. There had to be a silver lining in this news. Somewhere, however faint. They had found Thomas a ward bed and we found ourselves back in for the night. A scan was booked for the morning. I watched him sleep and I cried some more. I was drained of every bit of energy, but my mind wouldn't let me sleep. I hated that I couldn't fix it. That no amount of stamping my feet, asking questions or screaming at the sky was going to help.

I remember the date. November 14th, 2018. My next small room conversation with Dr Steve. Tom had completed the scan and had woken up from his anaesthetic. He was headache-free and feeling ok, playing on the iPad and enjoying visitors. He didn't seem too fazed that he was back in a hospital bed. Dr Steve said he had found a room that we could chat about the scan. Walking to the small meeting room, I thought – another small room. Look at all of those people waiting for us. Some I hadn't met before. There was no good news here. Only bad news was coming our way. I was shivering – the hospital air conditioning in the corridor was always too cold for me and I remember wishing I had grabbed a blanket. The small room was even colder.

Dr Steve had that face on again. I was expecting that face, but I thought I already knew the bad news. I thought he'd just be confirming what they saw on the first scan. We waited patiently for him to go through what they had found. Dr Steve was choosing his words very carefully. He was looking at us but also looking down as he formulated each phrase. His suspicions from the previous day were correct. The tumour was back but there was more. This tumour was now aggressive. It was positioned directly adjacent to Tom's brain stem, not far from where it had first been found. Not only was the tumour back but the rate of growth was tremendously fast. Just two months prior, there had been no tumour. Now it was the almost the same size as when Tom had first been diagnosed last year. Even worse though was the fact that Tom's tumour had metastasised. There was one large tumour but this time it was accompanied by multiple small tumours throughout his brain and spine. These would be growing too. And for every small tumour there were 3-4 microscopic tumours that would be growing but too small to see yet. Surgery would not fix it this time around. There would be little chance of resecting all of the tumours, Tom would be in a lot of pain following surgery and the likelihood of even more extreme brain injury was high. It wouldn't cure him and there would be little chance of any quality of life.

Dr Steve's final statement was, "I'm so sorry, Thomas is not going to survive this". All of this time, I had been leaning forward on the edge of the seat, holding my breath and I don't remember talking. I heard him say this and while everything he said was leading up to this announcement, I was still stunned by those words. All of the breath left my body. I don't remember taking another breath, but I must have. I started to shake. Violently shake. They went to get Owen. I was left alone for a moment. I threw the tissue box across the room. Owen came in and I started to cry. To wail. I told him and we cried together. He caught me as my legs buckled and we sat on the couch holding on to each other with desperation. The night before I had thought the worst possible thing was repeating the whole year again. It wasn't. It hadn't occurred to me that this was a possibility. I had been so determined every single day that this wasn't in our future. There was no escaping it though, no matter how hard I wanted it to be, I had no control over this. Helplessness had reached a new level for me.

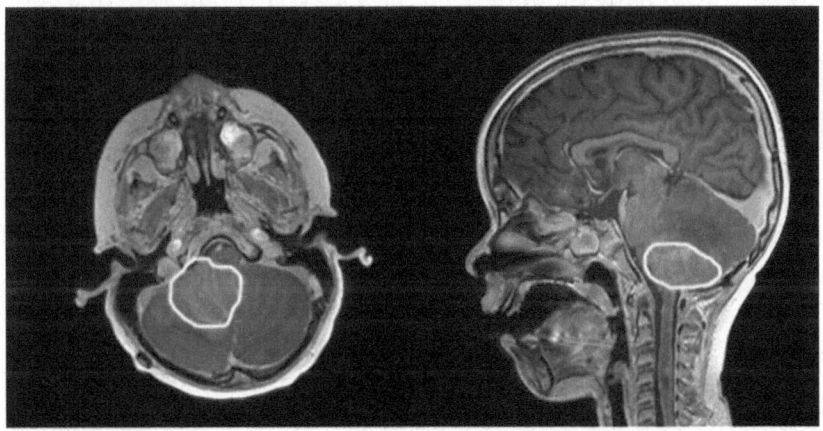

Images taken from MRI brain scan on November 14th 2018

Tom's new prognosis was terminal. The doctors were very surprised by this development – Tom's chances had been so good – this was so unexpected. I had lived for so long with the assumption that we would get through this – I had almost forgotten that children die from brain cancer. They die from it all the time. If we did nothing, we had days to weeks. If we did something, we had weeks to months. We needed more time and while none of the treatment would cure Tom, we would get a final Christmas, we would get another birthday if we were lucky.

I heard a song recently called **"Run So Fast"** by Missy Higgins that depicts my emotional state around this new conversation. I had believed in our treatment plan and in Tom's full recovery. Now, I was thrown back in that realm of despair, when for so long *hope* had been the guiding theme of our days. I was returned to a time of profound heartache and desperation. I didn't know how I would handle the ticking of this clock. What other hope is there if there is no hope for recovery? We had boldly declared that we were going to triumph, we had scoffed at the concept of failure. We were cocky and we got a slap across the head for it. 'Run so Fast' walks through my thoughts as if the songwriter had seen this path from hope to anguish.

Dr Steve laid out our options. He didn't recommend radiation and there were only three 2nd line chemo meds that were effective. One could be taken as a tablet and the other two were given intravenously. This would mean another surgery to insert a port-a-cath. A way into Tom's bloodstream but without the limitations of a central or PIC line. I was so worried about the side effects. How did we balance his treatment with his wellness? There was no proven method or combination that anyone could recommend. The more chemotherapy, the more chance of toxicity and side effects. The less chemotherapy, the less time. There was no winning formula and it was our decision.

After some very long discussions, the new treatment plan was agreed upon. We had decided to first try two of the medications: Temozolomide and Irinotecan. Thomas had been given dexamethasone after the discovery of the tumour to decrease the swelling around the tumour and to assist with pain and vomiting.

He would stay on this steroid for a time but be weaned off over the month. The combination of these drugs as a first cycle would hopefully give us a good chance at reducing the size of the main tumour and slow the growth of the rest. There was a plan to perhaps introduce a third drug – Avastin – in future cycles but for now this was our plan. These chemotherapy options were supposedly not going to impact Thomas as severely as the course he had during the year. So, the *hope* was that we would get some time and he would feel ok.

Over the next two months, we didn't know what to expect each day. There were times when Thomas would sleep most of the day away. His headaches continued periodically with some days a 'write off' as we focused on managing his pain with oxycodone and paracetamol. When days like these came along, fear would get the better of us. Imagining it was our last day, our last chance, set up a quiet state of panic. Last minute phone calls to photographers to capture images of Tom with his family. Visits to the park where Tom would be awake, fall asleep, be in good spirits, then frustration would take over. Posing for a camera when he could manage it. Letting him rest when it was all too much.

The first Monday of December, which was a couple of weeks after our new diagnosis, we had planned a trip to Stradbroke Island (fondly known as Straddie by the locals), a short trip off the east coast of South East Queensland. Thomas was tired on the barge and slept in the car, but this wasn't new. He slept through to the next morning. After that much rest, he should have been ok the following day, but Thomas wouldn't wake up. We had been taught that the sign of infection was a fever. If his temperature was elevated – head to the hospital. He had no temperature, but something was very wrong. He was wet with sweat but ice cold. The paramedics arrived and we found out Tom had something called 'cold sepsis'. An infection had taken over and he had to be airlifted back to Brisbane immediately. When being moved out to the ambulance Tom roused a bit but was in and out of consciousness. The urgency of the paramedics elevated my fears and the trip to the hospital was one of the most traumatic experiences of my life.

As Tom was airlifted to the hospital, we raced for the barge. I was shaking, crying and holding on with white-knuckled grip. I kept thinking: what if that was the last time I would see my son alive? What was the last thing I had said? How afraid must he be? Once on the barge my mind was going at a million miles an hour and in contrast we seemed to be barely moving in the water. I called Dr Steve but even his calm voice, listing the few positives he could wasn't enough to reduce my hysteria. The drive back from the dock to the hospital is usually an hour. We hit top speeds where we could, we ran red lights and swerved between lanes in crazed desperation. My frustration with any traffic in the way had me screaming at the top of my lungs. I got a call asking how far away we were. They were doing everything they could to keep Tom going until I got there. I had never felt that level of fear that hit my chest in that moment. I could see the hospital, but I wasn't there yet. What if he was gone before I could get there?

A nurse met me at the front entrance to Emergency and I was sprinting. I lost a shoe, I hit a wall with my shoulder taking a corner. People were waiting for me at every corner to show me where to go. Thomas was in a new area of the hospital that we hadn't been to before. He was in an area of Emergency called 'Resus' which is the zone in Emergency for critically unwell patients. His bed was surrounded by countless doctors and nurses. The doctors had accessed his veins; his face was covered by an oxygen mask on high flow and his torso was peppered with heart monitor pads. Tom's blood pressure had dropped perilously low and so the doctors had given him adrenaline and other inotropes. These medications were given to contract his blood vessels and get Tom's heart to pump harder hoping to get his blood pressure up. I climbed into bed with him and cuddled him from behind. I helped hold the mask and I spoke quietly into his ear. I looked up and saw that lovely nurse Gabrielle. She was there holding Tom's head, looking at me. She had no words of comfort for me, but it was something to know she knew us, and she was there.

Thomas was crying and calling out under the mask. He was so scared. I was so scared. Out of my mind scared. My heart pinch was crushing my chest with such force I struggled to breathe. The doctors had reached the limit of pushing the adrenaline and it had to go off. Dr Steve was there again with his serious face staring down at me, outlining our options. If Tom's heart rate couldn't sustain decent pressure we had to decide what the next step was. Intubation, which is to put a breathing tube down his throat, was an option. This might increase Tom's blood pressure, but he'd need to be put under (general anaesthetic) for that. There was no guarantee that he would ever wake up. Or…don't intubate – but then he might die right then and there from cardiac failure. Another impossible choice to be made. All while Tom is calling out under the oxygen mask, his bed surrounded by more than fifty on-lookers. I'm holding him, my whole body shaking as we tried to decide what was less likely to kill my son. The trauma of intubation was not something we wanted for him and so we went with the plan of dropping the meds and hoping for the best.

Tom was most upset by the oxygen mask and so to calm him down we tried to lessen the flow of oxygen and make him more comfortable. Everyone was watching the heart monitors. I couldn't look up and so I just kept talking into Tom's ear quietly that it was going to be ok, we needed to calm down and the doctors were just trying to fix his body. I was right beside him, I loved him, I believed he could do this, I knew he was scared, I was scared too but we were together, and it was going to be ok. "I have you bubba, I have you Tom." I chanted these words over and over while we waited to see if Tom's blood pressure would maintain its level after withdrawing the adrenaline. The suspense was like nothing I have ever felt.

"When little people are overwhelmed by big emotions, it's our job to share our calm, not to join their chaos"

L.R. Knost

As he calmed down, he became quiet. I didn't know what the beeping machines meant. I didn't know if he was alive or dying. I couldn't look at anyone – I just looked at the back of Tom's neck, talking softly and trying to hide that I was crying. I don't recall having any perception of time or how long we waited to hear the news that Tom was coping. He wasn't getting immediately better but he wasn't getting worse. Tom's father was there, and gradually other family members arrived. They took turns at Tom's bedside. Owen was leaning over me, tears falling down his face. Everyone was crying. There was nothing for it – there was no stopping it. I can't imagine how Thomas must have felt surrounded by all those who loved him, crying and telling him how loved he was. Eventually, the doctors' made the call that Tom had stabilised. He was to move to the Paediatric Intensive Care Unit for continued monitoring and treatment. I watched as the main doctor 'handed over' to the multitudes of people. At Intensive Care handovers it is crucial to give concise and accurate information so only the doctor handing over talks so that everyone can hear. There were student practitioners, registrars, consultants, nurses, all types of staff standing there – listening to the clinical account of Tom's case. None of this was clinical to me. I was on a wire over a very deep chasm holding on to my baby and praying for a miracle.

Thomas went into the Paediatric Intensive Care Unit and family hovered in the corridors and the family room. Once Tom was out of that initial state of crisis a strange type of reality returned. I watched while a doctor inserted an 'arterial line' into Tom's wrist. She stitched the line into the flesh of his skinny little wrist. Tom didn't jump as she pushed the needle into his skin, so I presumed some sort of anaesthetic was in play. He had become lethargic and so the staff had obviously medicated him as well. Upon arrival, Tom had been given the full gamut of life-saving medications, including another high dose of dexamethasone. He had been on this steroid for a few weeks by this point and with this extra hit, Tom was in for something new.

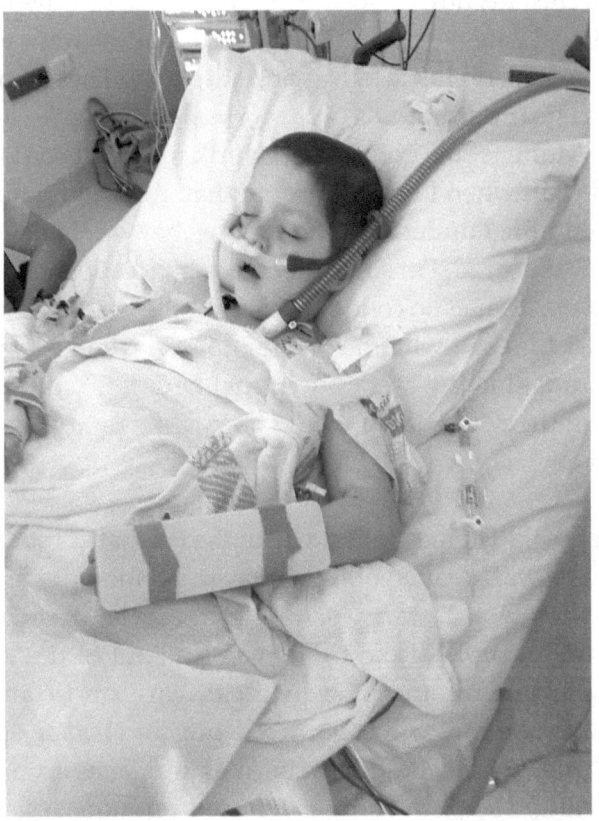

As Tom returned to full consciousness and took in every tube and bandage that covered him, he became angry. Angry like I had never seen. I recalled a conversation about 'dex' with one of the parents of a child with leukemia. Dexamethasone is given to those kids for a month at the start of their therapy. After 2-3 weeks of being on that steroid they go 'feral'. I understood that to mean they became grumpy, refused to do what they were told, etc. I was wrong. What

I saw was very different. The hormonal impact of this steroid was intense, and it broke my heart to see Tom change in such a short space of time. Just hours before, I had held him and thought he might die. My love for this boy was at full throttle and I wanted to show that any way I could. But all Tom had for the world was rage.

To his parents, his nurses, to anyone who came near he would say things like, "I hate you. I want to kill you. I never want to see you again". The look on his face was absolute fury. These words were difficult to hear but nothing was worse than when he said, "Just let me go Mum, let me go!" I didn't think my heart could be more shattered than when I heard him say that. All I could do was say that I loved him, I understood how angry he was. I knew it hurt; I knew he was scared. I'm sorry all of this had happened. That was all I could do. He had no control over anything that was happening. I had to let him say what he needed to say even as terrible as it all was. I imagine if it were me in that bed, hooked up to every machine in the world, that I would have some pretty nasty things to get out as well.

The doctors said Thomas would stay in the Paediatric Intensive Care Unit until he was weaned off the inotropes (blood pressure meds) and that they would start weaning him off the dexamethasone too. Within a couple of days, Thomas was out of the Paediatric Intensive Care Unit and on a medical ward on IV antibiotics. They couldn't be sure why it occurred, but Tom had an aggressive bacterial infection. It could have been as simple as a small tear in his gut lining, complicated by a depleted immune system. Often patients with sepsis like Tom can spend weeks in Intensive Care, but he made remarkable improvement and rallied far better than any doctor could have predicted. Tom's sweet nature returned after a few days as well. We talked with Tom about how scared he was, about how much pain he had been in when he said those things. I knew he didn't mean them; I knew he loved me and that it was the medication that put him in that state. I was still so relieved that he had survived the infection that nearly took him from me.

It was around this time and the months that followed, I started to notice the different ways people were behaving around me. I saw varied reactions from people once I told them about Tom's recurred cancer and what it meant for his future. I realised that there were four types of people:

- They who give you sad face
- They who avoid and go missing
- They who need a job
- They who are present

They who give you 'sad face' – I know when some people looked at me, all they could see was that my son was dying. They didn't necessarily see this in my face or my actions but that was the new identity I wore, in their view. I understand that it is a very normal reaction to then interact with me in that new frame. They grimace, they pat your back, and in their eyes is a very clear expression of… pity. This pity isn't mean-spirited at all – I know that this is the effort to show compassion, to acknowledge how big this situation was for me to deal with. This, as a start to a conversation is one thing, but the constant 'sad face' wasn't a great help to me. I didn't need reminders of how shit everything was or how sad I should be at every minute. Sometimes a smile was what I needed more than pity.

Clichés are sometimes all people can think to say but depending on what I was feeling at the time, they weren't always helpful. Sometimes they were enraging; "God only gives us what we can handle", "What will be, will be", "There's a reason for everything", "At least Cam is ok", "What doesn't kill us makes us stronger". These are perhaps the wrong thing to say to a mum of a terminal child. I learned that I didn't like to be told where to find the silver linings. I had gotten very good at finding them in the past and I know people were trying to find the positive. I remember someone saying to me, "How are you today?" and I thought, that's a question I liked. It recognised that individual days could be hard or ok. I could answer for that day without explaining my yesterday or my tomorrow. The simplicity of adding the 'today' puts far less pressure on me than having to find a generalised answer about my wellbeing. This question gave me control. It gave me a chance to decide where the conversation would go. It could go somewhere, or I could shut it down.

They who avoid and go missing – I know that these people are too afraid of saying the wrong thing. They might be too upset personally, to deal with me. I get it, they think it's best to stay away. Luckily for me the people that I needed around me were there for me and didn't shy away. Try not to but if you need to remove yourself from watching a tumbling down world, just make sure you come back. Send a text or a card and be fine with getting no response.

They who need a job are a funny breed – I had a good percentage of close friends that fit in this category. Their best way to deal with someone in pain is to fix it and if you can't fix it, provide the wine, bake the lasagne, find some service that will make it somehow better, even if only for a fraction of time. At times it was difficult to find jobs to delegate. There was nothing I needed but to have my boy safe and healthy. But no one could give me that. So they make you frozen meals, host playdates for Cameron, offer to pick up your washing and they donate to your Go Fund Me page. But sometimes, there are no jobs.

Then there were *they who are present*. They followed my lead even though I didn't realise it at the time. We would speak about Tom, about my fear, about my devastation, about everything that hurt – if that's what I needed. If I needed to talk about something else, we would chat about inconsequential nonsense. They would allow me that break from the ragged emotion. The constant anticipatory grief that had been following me around for so long. They would listen and find ways to be thoughtful. They would think of their favourite memories of Tom and share them with me. They didn't make it about them, but I knew they would be there for whatever I needed.

ANOTHER SMALL ROOM

I saw all of these present themselves to me from Tom's terminal diagnosis through to the months well into my grief. These responses are completely understandable, completely fitting with human nature and all of them come from a good place. Everyone's intention is compassionate and full of love. I didn't take offense to people trying their best to comfort me. Some made it better, some made it harder. But it was always going to be hard. Ever since that small room on November 14th, life was going to be bloody hard. I knew people just wanted to be there for me, as I wanted to be there for Tom.

Practical Advice:

- Take a blanket or a jumper to any small rooms.

- Making impossible decisions…

    - Think about what you would want for you.

    - If your child is an appropriate age, consider asking the child what they think … if you would be ok with whichever answer they choose.

    - Does one option give any level of increased comfort?

    - Don't beat yourself up for decisions once they are made. Nothing is for sure and you are doing the best you can.

- Don't just look for fever if your child is immune-compromised. Cold sepsis is just as dangerous and looks like altered consciousness, ice cold to touch, sweating, etc.

- Don't take it personally when your child bites back and gets frustrated. I think of every swear word that I would be using if it were happening to me.

- Know that everyone is trying their best to help.

- <u>Supporters:</u> No clichés and don't push. Acknowledge it is shit and just be ready to help in whatever way they ask

- <u>Co-parents:</u> Lean on your support networks. Ask the social workers for help if family support is limited.

Chapter 7

Bucket List Days

... and a Conversation

After the shock of hearing about the return of Tom's 'egg' and its many companion eggs, I had to turn my attention to how to make it better. I couldn't fix it. I couldn't save him. I had to accept that my role had changed again, and I had to find a new goal to work towards and to hope for. I had to find a way to balance the bad with a whole lot of good. To find days when Tom was well enough to have an adventure. Any adventure that could light up his face, catch him up on being a kid again and create as many memories for him, me and our family as possible. I asked him one day – if he could do anything at all, what would it be? You might guess that he'd say ride a motorbike, swim with dolphins, or meet someone famous. Tom's response was, "Sit-ups. I wish I could do sit-ups." I had a chuckle and then I rephrased, "I don't mean like a challenge, more like…a fun thing to do". He came back with a negotiation for some extra time on the iPad. I had asked him this question before he knew what was coming.

One of the most important, yet heart-wrenching decisions to make when you discover that your child has a terminal prognosis is whether or not to tell them. Again, having never been in this position, I hit the books, the blogs, the websites, asked the staff at the hospital who dealt with this every day – looking for any advice. Some way to make the decision easier. The majority of my searching for answers came to the same outcome – it is better to be honest. In the experience of hospital staff, many children with terminal illness already know the prognosis but they don't know how to talk about it. They don't know if they are allowed to talk about it to their parents. A kind nurse named Karen once said to me that the crisis points we kept hitting like the Straddie emergency and the days when he wouldn't rouse for hours – these were ways his body was giving us clues. To 'catch us up' in case we didn't know. She said, "Kids like Thomas begin to realise that something is wrong with their body, that it feels different somehow and intuitively they know".

I was so torn. I hated the idea of telling him. I was sick of telling him bad news, of convincing him to endure another blood test, to spit out another vomit, to push harder getting out of his chair. It's the most hideous thing to do but I knew I had to tell him. We also had to tell Cameron. Cam was confused as to why Tom still had to visit the hospital. He was asking why his brother wasn't getting better – when was he going to be normal again? Cam was frustrated by the extra attention Tom was still getting even after the bell ringing. He had expected that day to be a return to the way things were. He was suspicious that we were hiding something. And he was right. You would think the frustrations would be coming from Thomas. None of these questions came from Tom. To me, Tom already knew. Tom went about his day but never asked why his rehabilitation had stopped and why we were only doing fun things now.

I also watched the boys' relationship suffer. They were both impatient with each other, couldn't agree on things and preferred to play separately. If I were to continue to hide the truth from both of them how was Cam going to look back on that last period of time with Tom? What guilt would come from last fights or wasted time? How would these last memories stick when he didn't understand the significance of each day that we had left? Also, to think that Tom might not get the opportunity to say or do things that were important to him before he ran out of time. Yet another horrific decision to make but there was only one opportunity to get it right. So I made the call to tell Thomas and Cameron and this conversation was one of the hardest things I've ever had to do.

Then came the nitty-gritty. I had the why in my head but...what words do I say? Where, when and how? We decided to wait until after Christmas and split up the news into separate conversations. The first would be about the fact that the egg, the tumour, was back. This explained why Tom wasn't getting better. The second was about the terminal diagnosis and the third would be about legacy and memory-making. We went to parks for each chat – the first to Southbank in a large lawned area under a tall poinciana tree. We used to visit that spot when we would break out of hospital and lay down blankets to roll around on the ground. We'd look up at the sky, make faces for the camera and Tom would practice his floor work physiotherapy. I used to see that spot and smile. I don't anymore.

We told the boys separately, first Thomas and then Cameron. My memories of that first talk are fuzzy. Thomas was more focused on going for a swim. Once he understood what we were saying, he seemed disappointed that he'd still have to visit the hospital. His eyebrows didn't go fierce though. He accepted it, the way he had accepted everything that had come before. I had made a deal with myself not to cry. If I cried, it might make it harder for him.

I've seen fear on Tom's face before. It was during a visit to the Wet'n'Wild waterpark, nearing the end of the day and we had decided on two more rides – Lazy River and Mammoth Falls. My 'speed demon' Tom loved to race ahead in Lazy River, an attraction which most people happily float along on their tubes being carried by the current. But Thomas had pushed ahead and left the 'Lazy River' before us. He headed to the next slide on our list thinking he'd lost track of time and we would be there waiting for him. We were still looking for him on the River and for a short time, Tom was missing. He'd gone to Mammoth Falls, but we weren't there. He'd forgotten the plan to go to the 'bag spot' if he lost us and so Tom headed to check if the car was still in the carpark. I had contacted security and was trying to keep calm but with every minute that passed I grew more and more anxious. Owen headed off to Mammoth Falls and on the way back he saw Tom through the fence. He was in the carpark, walking back with a security guard. I remember his face as he came around the corner with Owen and saw me. My relief was overwhelming but seeing his scared little face broke my heart. His bottom lip was wobbly, his eyes were wide, eyebrows up high and he was trying not to cry. I ran straight to him for a big hug and we talked over what had happened. He rarely strayed too far after that day. I thought I might see that face in the park that day. I didn't see fear, he was calm. He didn't ask questions; he just took it in and asked to go to the pool.

Cameron was confused about the return of the egg, "But he rang the bell!" In Cam's mind, the whole cancer thing had finished that day in September with the ringing of the bell. Tom just had to get his legs back, his strength back and things would be back to the way they were. Once he understood, Cameron was also keen to shut down the conversation and focus on the next thing, the pool. We expected a bigger response I guess but they had both adapted along the way and this was just another bit of news to deal with. It wasn't something they could change, and it wasn't something that they wanted to talk about, so they changed the subject. Kids are amazing that way, but I thought perhaps the questions would come later once it all sunk in.

I was a wreck about the next conversation. I ran it over and over in my head and couldn't once do it without breaking down. I had figured out what I would say but I didn't know exactly how the boys would react and what questions would come. This time we went to a different park. A park where we'd never been and could easily never go to again. As we arrived I realised that I had been there before, years ago. Since Prep, the boys had been separated at school into different classes. A lot of the time, when party invitations were distributed amongst their classmates, both boys would get an invite regardless of whether they were in Tom's or Cam's class. But sometimes, for smaller parties, only one twin would be invited along. This particular birthday was a BMX party. Kids were asked to bring their bikes and helmets and the park had a gravel skate park with bike ramps and paths. Neither of the boys had been very keen on riding bikes and at the time, Tom still had trainer wheels on his. Tom took a few tumbles and, lacking confidence for the tallest ramp, decided to stay on the surrounding bike tracks. Well, here we were again at this park. I had packed a picnic and I kept having brief flashbacks to that hot day years before. When everything was simple, when my Tom was just like every other boy there, riding and running and playing.

We found a table in the shade and Owen took Cam for a run on the skate park and over to the playground while Tom stayed behind, wheeled up to the table. Tom wasn't keen on this; he wanted to join the fun with his brother. He apparently had no fear of the ramps anymore. In the week prior, Thomas had recently started to blow raspberries when he didn't like something or sometimes just to be funny. You'd ask a question or tell him what we needed to do, and he would poke out his tongue and blow a raspberry right at you. It was also a way to get out of answering sometimes. I explained that we just needed to have a chat first and then he could go play. He blew me a raspberry. After reminding him of our previous conversation, we talked about the egg. The doctors had given us more information about the egg. They say this time the egg is too big. The egg is growing too fast. This time there is no way to fight it and win. The doctors say that this time, the egg, the cancer would take him away to heaven. There was some medicine that Dr Steve could give us that might slow it down to give us all more time, but it couldn't be cured.

Tom didn't say much. I acknowledged that this was so hard, that he was so brave, and it wasn't fair. I went on to say that it was his body that was losing the battle – not him. That his spirit was strong – the strongest the doctors had ever seen. Once in heaven, his soul would be free of the egg and his failing body. In heaven, he would walk, he would run, he would fly. His grandfather Poppy would be there to look after him. Our dog Casbah would be waiting for him to play with and he would spend every day having the most wonderful fun.

I continued, when kids die their spirits are extra bright. They only give the most special jobs to children in heaven. When Tom arrived he would be given a star. Every night he would shine it for us. We would know it was his by how bright it would be. We would find him, and we would talk to him about our day, remind him how much we loved him and that he would still be a part of our lives and he would be able to watch out for us. Then I told him a story.

There was a man called Mr Hedgehog. He lived in a grey house and he wore a grey suit. He had a grey job and he had a grey face. Every day he went to work in his grey car and came home again at night. But he hadn't always been 'grey'. When he was younger he had such colourful dreams. He wanted to swim in the ocean, fly in a plane, ride a horse and climb the tallest mountain. He was older now and he had never done these things. Instead of the 'colour' of dreams, he had chosen a grey life.

On his way to work one day, he felt different. Something was wrong. He felt pain in his arm and his chest. Suddenly he realised he was having a heart attack. Suddenly he realised that he was in real trouble. Suddenly he realised he was out of time and he was going to die. It wasn't fair, where was his warning? In a rush, every colourful dream he used to have flashed into his mind. He felt such regret that he hadn't done these amazing things, that he had instead settled for the grey.

Then I said, "Tom this is the worst news, I know. But...something we must consider is that the doctors have given us this warning. We don't know how much time, but we have some. So now is the time to live those colourful dreams. Have some wonderful fun, make some wonderful memories – with us, with Cam, with everyone who loves you."

I stopped and asked Tom if he had any questions. He said, "So, I'm going to die when I'm a kid?" I replied, "Yes Tom. That's what the doctors have told us." He thought for a moment. I wanted to fill the silence – I was so scared of what he would say next. But he didn't say anything. He just blew a raspberry. We checked again if he understood and he nodded. Then he started to wheel himself away, towards Cam and Owen racing around the skate park. He looked back at us with this cheeky expression, checking he wasn't in trouble for leaving and then continued on his way. I knew that he'd already figured it out, before our visit to the park. He knew he was dying and there was nothing more to say. But for him, on that day...there was a skate ramp waiting in the sunshine so he was off to go have some fun.

We called Cam over to have a snack and some water. He came running across and while he nibbled away we started to have the same conversation. Cam's response was very different this time around. His disposition changed immediately. "Quick we have to go to the hospital! They have to fix it!" His concern and confusion were so heartbreaking but also so wonderful to see how much he loved his brother. He made every suggestion he could think of to tell the doctors how to fix it and we had to knock down each one. I didn't want the boys to consider there were multiple spreading tumours. That detail was so upsetting to me and so I didn't add that to our conversation. Cameron couldn't believe there was nothing to be done. Couldn't believe that we had to accept that Tom was going to die in a matter of weeks or months.

After that day I watched Thomas and Cameron's relationship change. Cameron had been pulled out of school and Thomas removed from his rehabilitation appointments weeks before. Thomas had more patience for Cameron. The impact of the dexamethasone had started to wear off and Tom returned to the kind boy that I knew. Cameron's need to win or grasping for more attention vanished. The boys had always loved to wrestle on the bed. I had put a stop to it once Tom was home because I didn't want Tom to be hurt and sometimes young boys don't always know the line. 'All fun and games until someone loses an eye.' One day on the couch, the boys were both in their pyjamas and they started to wrestle. Tom had reached out and was lying on his side grabbing at Cam. Cam could have moved away but instead put himself in the firing line and allowed Tom to have the upper hand. Cam pretended to be losing. He cried out in laughter, "Stop Tom, you're too strong!" I watched him give power back to his brother. Cameron gave Thomas a 'win' like the wins he'd had before all of this cancer rubbish had happened. I was so proud of Cam that day and in the days that followed. He showed me time and again how much he cared about his brother. I hope Cameron knows how thoughtful and beautiful those small acts were. The snippy little fights stopped, the frustration and competition stopped. They both had settled and were happily co-existing with more kindness than before.

 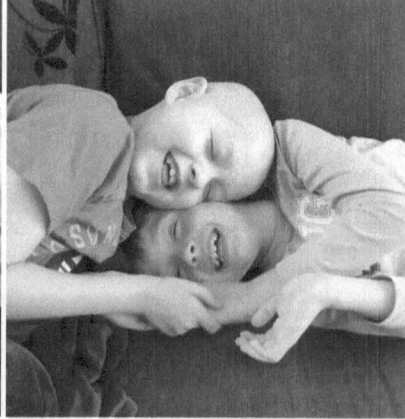

BUCKET LIST DAYS

We had started plans for memory-making not long after Dr Steve had given us our news. Between port-a-cath surgery, time in hospital, the cold sepsis and our weekly check-ups, we had to find time to build in some adventure. Some wonder and joy and fun and laughter. It was over these 'bucket list days' that I also learned how kind my community was. Months before when we were still oblivious of what was to come, my friend Danielle and her family had organised a fundraising event for me. I had stopped teaching nine months earlier and my family and friends were concerned about my finances. So, they organised a 'Superhero Trivia' night attended by more than 200 people and full of prizes, games and lots of champagne. I spoke to everyone about Tom's courage and how overwhelmed I was with the support of everyone in the room. Once November 14th came and went, we decided to set up a Go Fund Me page to raise funds for any experience Tom might want to request. I never expected such a response, but we raised over $36,000 for Tom's Adventures.

Our friend Trudi organised a special visit to the local police station where her brother worked. Thomas and Cameron were welcomed in and given special uniform shirts and hats and asked to be 'policemen for a day'. The boys were finger-printed and given a tour of the station. The station had arranged for the dog squad, the mounted patrol and the road police to attend that day. Tom received a beautiful toy German shepherd puppy in police garb which resembled the puppy-in-training "Punch" who he met at the station. We headed out to the car park and met two horses, "CJ" and "Kokoda". Cam got to jump on top of one horse and Tom gently stroked the other's big nose, happy to stay in his chair. The traffic control guys showed the boys how to use the radar gun and they tracked Cam's speed running across the car park. The boys insisted on breathalysing everyone at the station and then they were both offered a ride in their own police car.

Tom chose the dog squad car and they each got to ride in the front seat – this was a big deal for both of them, as they were

always relegated to the back seat as children. They asked if I was coming and I said, "No! I'm not a policeman – you are! This is your adventure!" Thomas was allowed to press every button and siren and Cam even had a go on the radio. The boys came back beaming from the excitement. The final activity was the motorcycle. We lifted Thomas up on to the stationary motorbike and he got to rev the

engine and sound the siren. He concentrated so hard and revved it as hard as he could. I seriously thought he'd cook that engine! It was revved to a maximum level and the noise alone was deafening. He loved every minute of it. The cops mirrored every opportunity for Cam, and it was a brilliant morning.

We came up with every fun thing we could find. We attended theme parks and as a family we made Christmas decorations. The four of us went out on the boat and Owen taught Tom how to fish. Cameron had already had a go at fishing on the boat months before and wasn't a fan of keeping the fish for dinner. The boys were looking into the bucket of fish and Tom was in a fit of giggles as Cam pretended to speak for the fish. "Let me go!" he would call out in a Kermit-like voice. So Tom learned to fish that day, pulling in some little fish and then ready to go again with a fresh line. He also got to sit up front and drive. Captain Tom's face was a picture of concentration for a while and then as Owen pushed the speed more and more, his face lit up with excitement. My little speed demon loved to go fast!

Fishing trip out on Moreton Bay, at the captain's wheel with Owen

We organised playdates with Tom's friends and visited our cousins up the coast. I wanted to surround Thomas with other kids. He had spent so much time in the company of adults at the hospital and so I needed him to feel like a kid again. Even just hanging out with other kids, watching telly, playing with nerf guns or Lego or just having fish and chips for dinner was something awesome in Tom's eyes. Any day Tom had the energy to swim we headed to the beach or the local pool. He preferred the pool, because it gave him independence. He was like every other kid. I remember the sunshine on those hot summer days. I loved that it was another gorgeous Australian summer and we were all together. I remember him swimming up to me for hugs and to escape the splashing when Cam was being thrown around the pool by Owen.

BUCKET LIST DAYS

Tom and I swimming in the wave pool at Wet n Wild waterpark

Camp Quality is a charity that provides amazing experiences for children with cancer. We attended a great family camp weekend up at Noosa. Family came to visit, and we played in the pool most of the time. We met some wonderful people and even though Tom was struggling with vomiting and diarrhoea as a result of his new chemo, it was a gorgeous weekend. We also made trips to the beach where Tom spent his time playing in the sand. Actually, more often than not he would give orders and design ideas of what we should build or dig in the sand.

In the May of 2018, my wonderful partner Owen had proposed to me. We had been out at dinner for my birthday and I remember us dancing with friends into the night. My face and my tummy muscles were sore from laughing so hard from the fun of it all. When making plans for our 'bucket-list days' I knew that I wanted Thomas to be there for our wedding. So with only a couple of weeks to plan – we got married! Thomas was newly out of hospital from the 'Straddie' infection and feeling better. The dexamethasone had left him puffy in his face and torso, but even so, he looked so dapper in his waistcoat and pants. His hair had been growing back during the previous months and so I was even able to get him a haircut – just to tidy it up a bit. I loved these little things we did to prepare. Even though his face was rounder, he was in his chair, and he still had a nasogastric tube taped to his cheek – I was so joyous that we had that day together.

Thomas, Cameron, Owen and I were surrounded by our family and friends. Tom found a smile, he ate cake, he signed our marriage certificate alongside his twin brother. The boys walked me up the path to find Owen by the garden. Tom's chair was decorated with poinciana flowers and baby's breath to match those in my hair. After the ceremony, Thomas and I 'chair-danced' to his favourite song like the way we used to every morning in the car. I had asked an art teacher friend to prepare a canvas for us that day. It had the outline of a bare tree in black marker. Chris arrived with the canvas stretched on a frame and came with a selection of various paints. Our guests were all asked to choose a shade of green and press their thumbprint onto the branches. Once the crowds had placed their 'leaves' it was our turn. We all chose a very different colour: Tom chose red for me and purple for Owen. Cameron chose teal and Thomas chose blue. This canvas still hangs in our dining room and it reminds me of that day.

We didn't have a lot of structure to our days – we had to play it by ear dependent on how Tom was feeling each morning. Any food he asked for, we got! But his appetite was starting to fade as the level of steroids dropped in his system. His levels of exhaustion started to increase as the days went by. We were faced with the difficulty of balancing his wellness and his capacity to enjoy each adventure. I knew we were running out of time and at times I felt it was all a bit too frantic – for him and for me. Most days I would have preferred to sit on the couch, bundled up with him in a blanket like we used to in the hospital. Or out in the garden sitting in the dappled shade listening to the birds and some tunes on a sunny afternoon. Each evening we had a ritual of night-time cuddles. Sometimes we would read or talk, take ridiculous selfies or listen to one of Cam's outrageous stories. But every night I'd have him folded under my wing for cuddles before bed. Before I had to worry about prepping his meds, attaching his feed pump or transferring him out of his chair. These cuddles became significantly precious in my memory-making with Tom. It was a time where he felt safe and I felt safe and it reminded me of the nights we did this before medulloblastoma, before posterior fossa and before I knew my baby was going to die.

The movie 'The Greatest Showman' had been released in 2017. I remember hearing the soundtrack and loving the main anthem of the film: **"This Is Me"**. When Tom was in hospital, we watched the film and then started listening to the songs during the morning commute. This song is about overcoming adversity, being brave and finding worth. I love the word 'glorious'. My good friend Sharon will often use the term and when I hear it in the song I immediately think of my Tom and his bravery. I watched my son transform over our year-long battle. He had lost his movement, his speech, his hair. He worked so hard to get these back. Every minute…Thomas was just…glorious. I saw his courage taking in the news about his terminal diagnosis. I watched him laugh and play despite all of it. He didn't lose his spark or feel sorry for himself. Thomas didn't let himself be grey even in face of every obstacle, every broken part of his failing body. He didn't focus his time on his limitations or his differences. I don't know that I could have been that brave. So as we went about making our memories together I was reminded of the message of this song and how it described Tom's character. How *fortunate to be the mother of such a boy.*

Practical Advice:

- The Difficult Conversation: It'll be one of the hardest things to do. Everyone has to make their own call as to whether they tell their child they are dying. I am glad I told my sons the truth. If you are struggling with the decision, I hope that our story is a help to you.

- People will show you enormous generosity when they hear of a child with terminal cancer. We were offered the police station day, backstage access to theme parks, special rides in vintage cars and on quad bikes. When things can feel so bleak, it is so lovely to see such good in the world and how much people can give of themselves for the benefit of a child.

- Find ways to balance your need to do 'big ticket' memory-making with the simplicity of spending time together at home, in the quiet every day. I find those memories of cuddles and late night chats far more precious now.

- Tom couldn't always do everything. We had a little time... but he was still sick. We had to allow him the chance to rest. Balance the fun with proper rest time so your child can actually enjoy these adventures.

- If you want protected time with your sick child, don't be afraid to say no to visitors. You might find them lining up with invites or 'pop-ins' but if you need time alone, you can make that call.

- <u>Supporters:</u> If you have contacts who might be able to offer an awesome experience – lean on them. It doesn't have to be money – some of the best things we did with Thomas were through our mates getting creative.

- <u>Co-parents:</u> Some split families might be able to do joint memory-making, and if so – great! Some might only handle creating memories as separate families. Wanting time alone with your child is a reasonable thing. Not every minute can be yours even though you are desperate for every minute left. For us it worked to formulate a two-night turnaround schedule, text each other with information about how Tom managed each day and just enjoy the time we had with him.

Chapter 8

The 'Pal' I Never Wanted

Palliative Care

Dr Steve had booked an MRI following the first cycle of 2nd line chemotherapy once Thomas had recovered from the Straddie infection. The combination of the dexamethasone and the chemotherapy drugs showed a 50% reduction in Tom's tumour. I couldn't believe it, I thought about how much time we would have, I thought what if this actually worked and Tom's body was able to keep up the fight. My delight turned to apprehension as I was struck by the look on Dr Steve's face – which was still fixed in 'small room mode'. Why wasn't he thrilled? Wasn't this good news? He assured me this was good news, but I was wary of getting my hopes up. Perhaps he had seen this before and he could already predict the outcome of the next scan. Perhaps this was a precursor to something bad. So, I took it all in with a sense of unease.

Weeks prior to this new MRI we had met Karen, a nurse from the Palliative and Pain Team. She was softly spoken, attentive and compassionate. I often thought to myself with each new person I met in response to Tom's battle – what a horrific job they had. Every day dealing with dying children, grieving and sometimes angry parents. Even the paediatric oncology staff – surely the loss of children in their care, time after time starts to tear at the edges of your soul. I asked Dr Steve and Karen why they did the job. Dr Steve said to me that while it was definitely a rollercoaster, the good outcomes made up for the sorrowful. And I could see there was a sense of purpose – I felt very lucky to have someone like him to steer us through this. We need people willing to care for our kids when they are this sick, when they are too sick to continue. Karen said to me that while her job was certainly difficult at times, it was also very rewarding to see the love of families and the beautiful soul of each child at peace towards the end of their fight. I had read a book called 'Follow The Child', by Sacha Langton-Gilks. She insists that a terminal diagnosis doesn't mean you have given up hope. It means you now must hope for something else. Your hope for your child's future becomes a hope that if they must die, they can do so in the most peaceful way possible. So, this became my hope.

I remember those times throughout 2018 in the hospital where the word palliative was a terrible word. I had always recoiled at the thought of it. Palliative was meant for the old man, not the seven-year-old boy. But when you have the new nightmare of a terminal cancer prognosis come into your life, you need all the support you can get. So Karen met us and talked us through what their team provided. We were given a 24-hour number to call for…anything. For advice on meds, for medical questions, for help with equipment, for appointment making, for a chat or a cry…anything really. I called them the 'Pal Team'.

The Pal Team had a focus – to give Tom whatever he needed. To manage his pain if, or when it came and to do so with decent meds that gave him quick relief. To assist with arrangements surrounding our memory-making – for example to ensure Thomas was comfortable and able to attend and enjoy our wedding. As outpatients we had new rules and we became a top priority. No more waiting in the 5C oncology clinic waiting room. Straight in for numbers and straight into a bed. I remember a day when Thomas was getting his obs done: blood pressure, temperature, etc. He asked the nurse for a sticker and said, "Actually maybe I could have two? I'm dying you know. Not today, but I'm dying". He said it so matter-of-factly.

The Pal Team were there just as much to support me as to support Thomas. Karen talked me through a lot of the heartache surrounding the future we were lined up for. She talked about the close calls Thomas had suffered. She said these things often happened with terminal children as a way of preparing us, getting us ready. I was able to talk through what I had planned to say to the boys in our grim conversations and she supported my decision all the way. Karen gave us some beautiful ideas for memory-making and always had a smile for Tom even though at times he had just had enough of meeting new nurses and making conversation. Then the eyebrows would drop down and the responses turned to raspberries.

Karen also told me that children in Tom's position would start to give us little gifts. Kids are just so amazing and sweet, and it becomes important to them to give peace to their parents. My boys and I were always very affectionate. Lots of kisses, cuddles and "I love you". During our night-time cuddles both at home and in the hospital Thomas started to give me his little gifts. He said things like, "You're my love, you're my adorable". His "I love you" expanded into, "I love you as far as the planets and the whole galaxy and the moon". When asked what his favourite things were, he replied, "My favourite thing is playing games and puzzles with you". My favourite thing was when we would just lie on our sides facing each other and he would stroke my cheek. Tom would be so gentle, and I would tell him, what a wonderful feeling it was when he did that

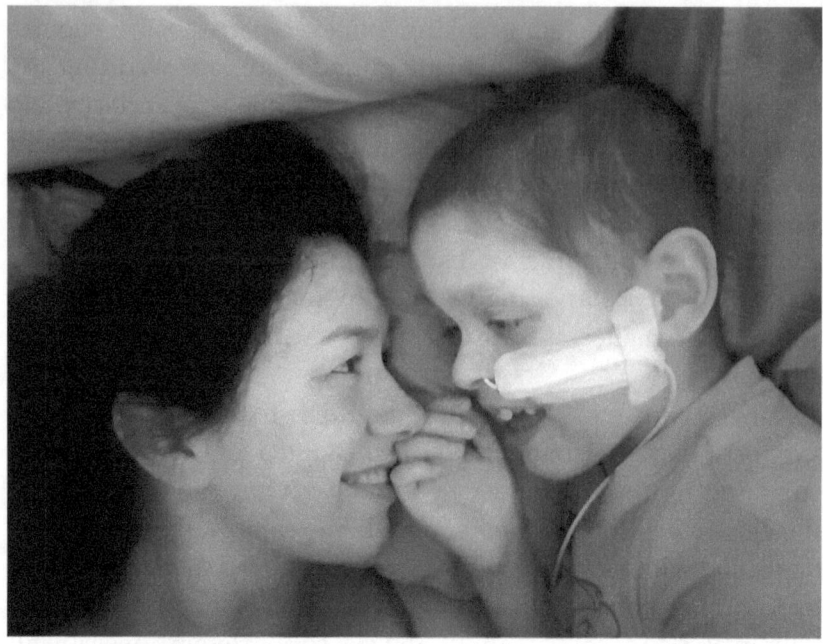

for me. I remember in the car, he started to hand over his title of Spotto champion. Rather than call out, "Spotto!" he started to say, "yellow". I asked what he was doing, and he said he was giving Cam and me his sightings without taking the points. "I'm giving you clues, that way you can win".

The boys loved the animated movie 'Trolls'. They quoted their favourite lines, talked about their favourite scenes and listened to the music. One song on the soundtrack became a favourite of mine as we listened to it over and over. **"True Colours"** had never been a standout song for me before, it's a bit cheesy I guess, but the duet version of this song in this movie is so beautiful to me. The scene in the movie shows one character trying to convince another of their worth. They comfort their friend even though they are in the same predicament and place of despair themselves. When I listen to that song, particularly that version, I think of Tom and how he provided that comfort for us in his final weeks. This song also reflected what I saw in him – his thoughtfulness, his worry for me, his patience. He was in that mindset perhaps where there was nothing else to do but give peace and love to his family, and so he did. There were times when he was quiet and perhaps he was in a moment of sadness. But he didn't spend his days crying or acting out. His 'colours' weren't distorted by anger or dimmed by sorrow. Instead I saw him smile, I felt him stroke my face and I heard him tell me how much he loved me.

We attended a family New Year's Eve party on the Gold Coast. There were rides, junk food, glowsticks and glow toys as well as a live band and a big oval for the kids to run around. Tom was unable to go on the faster rides, so I took Cam and Owen stayed with Tom. One of Owen's favourite memories with Tom was that evening. We'd bought spinning glow toys that, once Tom got going, were an absolute delight. He giggled and squealed. The look on his face that night remains with Owen and still brings him to tears. The countdown for New Year's Eve was set for 9pm so that families could get children off to bed but still enjoy the fireworks. Tom had a marvellous time with his glowing 'lasers' and as the sun went down, the boys wrestled on the picnic blankets. They giggled and Cam took on the play-victim role in the competition. The day had taken its toll though and Thomas was exhausted by about 8:30pm. He couldn't keep his eyes open and so he settled down to sleep before countdown.

Over the following week, Tom's energy continued to diminish, and his headaches started to return. Sometimes Panadol helped, sometimes long naps were the answer. "Follow the Child" by Sacha Langton-Gilks was a book I had found which focused primarily on options within palliative care and providing the best end-of-life care for a dying child. I had been looking for any book that had any similarity to what we were going through. Parts of it were enormously helpful to me. The first chapters were about the importance of the 'conversation'. The rest of the book was about what the final weeks and days would look like for a child dying of brain cancer. I started to see the descriptions from those chapters presenting in Thomas. His lethargy, his waning appetite, his increasing pain. I knew we were running out of time and it was only January. When they said months I was hoping for closer to ten, not two. On Sunday night, the 6th of January 2019, Thomas suffered terrible headaches throughout the night. He was due for a hospital check-up the following morning and so we wanted to follow this up with the doctors.

Tom was feeling very rough that morning. He was tired and upset from dealing with constant pain which Panadol and even oxycodone hadn't really improved. As the nurse came to wheel Thomas into the main area of the Day Clinic, I was walking behind them down the narrow corridor. He said to me, "Mum, I think I'm gonna die soon". Thank goodness he couldn't see my face at that moment. I was crushed. He knew and he was just telling the truth. No melodrama, no fuss, just being honest about it. And I had absolutely no idea what to say. I couldn't speak. I had to hold myself together or I might have broken down and never got back up. The nurse said to him, "Oh precious" but other than that all we could do was continue our journey to his treatment bed. His exhaustion took over as we lifted him into the bed and the pain meds started to take effect.

Dr Steve came in and saw that Tom's oxygen was too low, his colour wasn't right, and he struggled to rouse. Tom was placed on oxygen and Dr Steve arranged an emergency MRI to see what was happening inside. Tom slept through the whole thing and was then moved to a ward bed while we awaited the results. Eventually, Dr Steve came to collect us, and we left Tom in the capable hands of friends and family. I already knew what was happening. We were walking to our last small room. One more conversation with Dr Steve which would shatter our existence once again.

Karen wasn't there but another palliative nurse, Leanne, was in the room to help Dr Steve. We didn't know but before we entered that room, plans had been put in motion. Dr Steve informed us that the tumour had grown aggressively since Tom's previous scan and

THE 'PAL' I NEVER WANTED

was moving in a bad direction. It was now pressing hard against the brain stem. We asked, "How long?" He hesitated. "Days or maybe a week." We asked, "Will he make his birthday?" "I don't think so, he might but I don't think we have that long." The nurse chimed in with plans to manage his pain and to deal with other logistics. Thomas had vomited up his nasogastric tube the night before and the nurse questioned whether or not it should be left out now. That hit me in the chest. My father had passed away just over 18 months before and I knew what that meant. I said, "If he doesn't have the nasogastric tube, he doesn't eat. That's not a week, that's days!" I said this…with force. Dr Steve and the nurse could only look at me. I realised; this talk of a week was merely a kindness. They were suggesting it could be a week but they knew better. It was much closer than that. This would be his last Monday. He'd just had his last weekend. My heart pinch was in full gear as the reality of it all sunk in.

I insisted that they return his tube so that he could at least have water and they agreed. I asked about his medications and they said that there was no reason for him to have them anymore. Instead they were going to insert a temporary access point in his thigh for instant pain management. That I didn't have to worry about doses

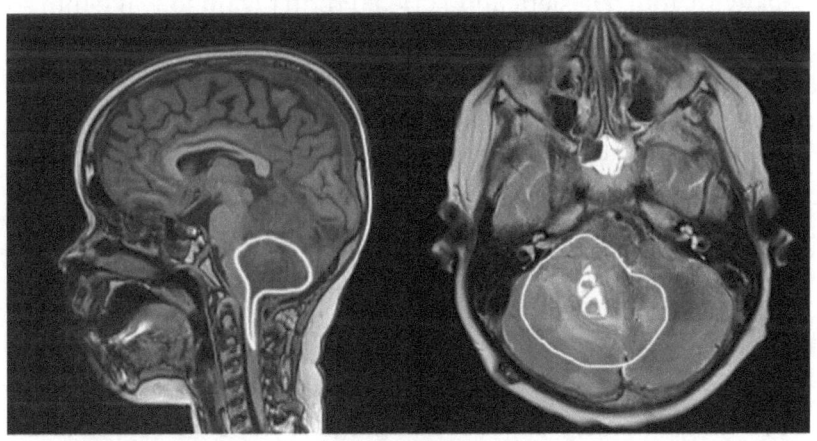

Images taken from MRI brain scan – January 7th 2019

too much, the important thing was to keep Tom comfortable. I wanted to take him home, but we needed a plan. I didn't want him to die in hospital and so I asked about availability at the children's hospice. They had already booked us in for tomorrow and we were free to spend tonight at home together.

The nurse showed me how to administer morphine into his leg and gave me the 'medical toolbox' to take home. It was an actual toolbox. Full of pain meds and anything else I could need. The Pal Team had become the Pain Management Team. The 24-hour number was listed, and Leanne told me to call if I was worried about anything – no matter what time, no matter how small. She gave me instruction for what to do if he passed away that night. "Call the ambulance but then have them call me and I will sort everything out from there," she said. Tom was too tired to sit anymore and so we planned to have him lie along the back seat with his head on my lap. They handed me a letter to show police if we were pulled over for any reason. They had thought of everything. They had done this before, and they were calm. I tried to be calm, but I was falling apart inside.

I remember that drive home. Owen was driving and I was in the back with Tom. He slept and I cried. I didn't want to wake him so I silently, but violently, cried. I put my head back and let the tears stream down my neck and onto my shirt collar so they wouldn't land on Tom's perfect face. He was still on oxygen; his breathing was slow but he was as comfortable as we could make him. Between my sobs I would look down at my beautiful, blameless boy and feel such devastation in my chest. It was happening and I was so scared. How did I make this ok for him, how could I help, how could I watch him die? I only had one chance at this, and I had to find a way to cope.

Once we got home, I didn't even have to say to Owen that he'd be on the couch that night, so Tom and I could have our last night-time cuddles at home. As I changed Thomas into some fresh, soft clothes he woke up and had a bit of energy. He was pretty happy to be sleeping in bed with me that night but we stayed up a little longer to talk. I took some videos that night while we talked. He wanted to tell me about the different Christmas presents he had chosen for Cam and his half-sister Lula. I told him how kind and thoughtful he was. He said that he loved making Christmas decorations and asked if we could make some tomorrow and I said I would love to. He asked me to smile at the camera, he stroked my cheek and he got annoyed at the oxygen tubes that kept slipping off. The only time he got upset was when he talked about Cameron. He said, "I don't want to die before Cameron." I said, "I don't want you to die at all." I imagine how scary it would have been for him, knowing he was going alone. He had to find heaven on his own. And my heart broke all over again. How many times can your heart break? As Tom started to get tired, our chats slowed to a stop. I turned off the lamp and we were lying there in the dark. I went to turn off my video but halted when he spoke. The last thing he said to me that night was, "I love you Mum".

Practical Advice:

- Talk to your Palliative team about anything and everything. Vent to them, question them, ask for advice, cry on their shoulder. They have been here before and they have the best knowledge, skills and words for what to do and say to help you.

- Take videos and photos as often as you can. If you can't, ask your partner and other family members to surreptitiously do this for you. Memory-making is easier to hold on to if you have these images in the time that follows.

- There are three options for where someone dies: Hospital, Hospice or Home. Perhaps have a think about your preferences before it gets too close.

- Take advantage of these gifts your child will give you and say things that you want to say in these last days.

- <u>Supporters:</u> Buy them the book "Follow the Child" by Sacha Langton-Gilks.

- <u>Co-parents:</u> Work together as best you can. This isn't about you – it's about your bub. Remember that you're both hurting and do the best you can to support your child.

Chapter 9

The Importance of a Hummingbird

End of Life Care

I didn't sleep at all that night; Tom's last night at home. I listened to him breathe, I held him and felt his thin legs and body fold into the shape of mine. A number of times, Tom stirred in discomfort, calling out and so I gave him morphine. I put small doses of water down his tube to keep him hydrated but eventually, all of it came up in a vomit. I had read that eventually his body would reject all food and fluids and it had started that process. My dread and my panic were building. The next morning we packed for our move to the hospice for an unknown period of time. While Owen filled the suitcase and Cameron was trying to gather his toys, I was trying to wake up Thomas. After a time he roused, but he found it difficult to speak. When he could say a few words, he was confused and repeated the start of a sentence without finishing it. He had become incoherent and then silent and then he fell back asleep. Cam didn't understand what was happening at the time but later that morning it started to dawn on him that something was different. We moved Tom out into the living room to see if that helped with his ability to wake but he couldn't maintain alertness for more than a few seconds. I was so worried that the next time he wouldn't wake up. I called the Pal Team and described our night and Tom's difficulty with waking. The nurse on the other end of the line listened and said to me, "Trish, this might be happening sooner than we thought. Come as soon as you can, and we'll sort things out once you're at the hospice". So we got in the car and drove.

Hummingbird House is the only children's hospice in the state of Queensland. In fact there are only three children's hospices on the east coast of Australia with Bear Cottage in New South Wales and Very Special Kids in Victoria. Current statistics estimate around 3,700 Queensland children are living with life-limiting conditions. The House provides short break stays, family support services, creative therapies, care at the end of life and after-death care, including grief and bereavement support (see Appendix 3 for further details about Hummingbird House). I didn't understand how Hummingbird House could accommodate us with such little notice, but I learned that emergency visits were part of their brief. They always kept space for families like ours.

Thomas slept on my lap all the way to the House and Cameron travelled in with my mum. Once Thomas was settled into his room, I climbed into bed with him. There I stayed, and but for one trip to the loo, I was by his side from that point on. Both sides of our family, mine and his dad's, were there. Family members came and went through the day as Tom slept. For a small amount of time Thomas woke and was calling out in pain. The nurses administered more pain relief and from then he settled. We were told that Thomas wouldn't wake again. The day was to be spent talking to him, holding him and saying our goodbyes.

THE IMPORTANCE OF A HUMMINGBIRD

Cameron floated in and out of the room. Upon arrival, watching all of the adults and noticing the mood in the room, Cam came to me and asked if Tom was about to die. "Soon bubba, maybe today, maybe tonight or tomorrow. This is our chance to say goodbye." Cameron tried to keep himself busy and wanted to find ways to help. On his iPad he created pictures using a landscape app to spell out letters. He made a scene that showed a T for Thomas and then added a C for Cameron. One by one he created more scenes that included everyone who was there that day. He sat on the bed with us sometimes and other times he played in the garden outside.

We were told that hearing is the last sense to fail and that Thomas could hear what we were saying. I talked softly to Tom, right next to his ear. I spoke of my favourite memories, about all the things he meant to me and how strong he was. I talked about how amazing heaven would be and how much fun it was going to be to run and fly. The advice I had been given said that it was important to let Thomas know that it was ok to stop fighting. Children often linger in an effort to protect their parents who don't want to let them go. I whispered to him, that he had fought for so long, but he could rest now. Whenever he was ready, he could go. That he could visit me in my dreams and that he would shine his star for us. Throughout the day I held him, I hummed our favourite melodies, I stroked his cheek memorising every contour and how soft his skin was against my fingertips.

Tom's breathing and heart rate started to become less rhythmic. He wasn't attached to any monitors or tubes anymore. The doctors had removed his nasogastric tube and the nasal prongs for his oxygen. I was so worried that at any moment he would slip away from me and I might miss it if I wasn't paying attention. Weeks before as I vented every fear I had in my heart at poor Karen. I mentioned this anxiety I had about not being there when my Tom left. She said that every mother she had worked with, every mum who had lost a child, they knew when it was coming. She said that a mum's physical connection to her child was still as strong as when that baby was growing inside her. She told me not to worry, that I would instinctively know – but I kept thinking – I only get one chance.

Thomas was still with us that Tuesday night when we turned off the lights. One lamp stayed on and I was tucked in beside him in his bed. He was wearing his favourite Bumblebee transformer shirt and I was holding his hand. I hadn't slept the night before and I was emotionally fatigued from the significance of that day. I kept drifting off in the low lit, quiet room and would get a fright each time I awoke. Had I missed it? Was he gone and I was asleep? I knew the guilt would haunt me, but my eyelids continued to droop. The only noise in the room was the sound of Tom's breathing. It was slightly ragged and shallow but thankfully it didn't have the rattle that can sometimes come. He sounded and looked comfortable and for that I was relieved.

Something woke me in the middle of the night. I don't know if it was Thomas, a noise he made or a jerking movement, but I awoke with a start and I knew instantly that it was about to happen. His breath had changed. I told him I was here and it was all going to be ok. He took two deep breaths and then one tiny one. And then at 1:25am, Thomas was gone. I folded his limp body into my arms, and I felt myself break. No longer could I hold him, whisper to him, sing to him. Instead I wailed, I rocked, I squeezed him. My cries, my rocking – it was primal in its intensity. I screamed to the sky. It didn't matter that I had known it was coming. I was still so overcome with such pain and loss. I felt as if I would fly apart if I let him go. Agony is the appropriate word and a feeling that I don't believe I ever fully understood until that night.

Tom's father, my mum and I each spent time holding him and crying. When he wasn't in my arms I alternated between hysteria and numb disbelief. After a time we called the nurse and they organised to move him to the Hummingbird Suite. This was a room designed to keep Tom's body cold and delay any process of deterioration. Something surprising happened next. When we lay him down again on his pillow, his facial expression had changed. While asleep, Tom's mouth had fallen open but when we put him back down after holding him and carrying him close, his face had settled into this beautiful slight smile. I couldn't believe it; he looked so gorgeous and so at peace. I hadn't seen him so serene and it gave me comfort to think that this smile showed me his relief at the end of his fight. That look on his face continues to help me even now. As if it were a sign that there are better things beyond this world – at least for a young innocent boy like my Tom. I did wish him back again but for a time before that December of 2017. I was living a nightmare and I wished it all away a million times. I wanted to go back to before the tiredness, before the egg, before the treatment and rehabilitation and every difficulty that he was faced with. But I couldn't. We were here and he was gone and the best hope I had was that he was free of the exhaustion, the suffering and the fight.

So when I saw you sleeping

So peaceful, free from pain

I could not wish you back

To suffer that again

Anonymous

We learned more about the hospice in the coming days. We were given a key to Tom's new room and took turns through the week that followed visiting him. His bed had been lined with ice mats and you could hear the constant hum of the cooling system. I spent my time with Tom in the Hummingbird Suite, holding his hand, stroking his cheek, talking and singing to him. We listened to music, he listened to my stories of him as a baby, as a toddler, precocious memories of him and his brother up to mischief. I spoke of my loneliness, my sadness and he listened to me apologise for everything I had ever done wrong. Every day I would ask him what wonderful corners of the world he had been exploring that night. Had he marvelled at the northern lights over the ice? Did he enjoy sliding down the face of the pyramids into the sand? Perhaps he had discovered caves at the bottom of the ocean full of treasure or unknown creatures? Maybe he had travelled further and uncovered the mysteries of the night sky and the universe beyond.

I hoped he had found Poppy, his grandfather, as soon as he had arrived there. "Poppy will look after you and it's your job to keep Poppy on his toes. Poppy will race you," I said. "Because in heaven it doesn't matter how old you are when you get there, you can do anything. Poppy used to be pretty fast Tom, so you'll have to push hard to beat him across the finish line." I said, "there are lots of other kids in heaven, more than you would have thought. You'll have lots of friends. But don't forget me Bubba. Don't forget to watch over us. To visit me each night." I was missing him so desperately.

Sitting in that bedside chair, at first I would touch his face and hold his hands. They were icy cold but soft. Then he started to feel hard and I thought, what if I lose the memory I had of him, when he was warm and loose in my arms. So I stopped myself from touching him for a day or so. After a time though, I couldn't stop myself. I just wanted to climb in and keep him warm. To snuggle like we always used to. I held his hand again and stroked his cheek. Mostly I sat there and cried, for everything he should have had time to do, for the years taken from him and from me, for the unfairness, for the pain in my heart. For the world which had lost such a beautiful soul, his cheeky grin, his love of music and puzzling things out. I cried over the fact that I would never again feel his tight hug around my neck. Tom's godfather, my friend Ben, came to give a blessing and to say goodbye. Danielle also came to visit. Dan was my bridesmaid, Tom's godmother and the shoulder I would often cry on when things went wrong in my life. She walked into the suite with me, bundled in our blankets. I said her, "Isn't he so beautiful?" As a nurse Dan had seen all sorts of things in her work but that day she fell to the seat, broke down and wept.

We asked Cameron if he wanted to visit his brother in the Hummingbird Suite. He hesitated for a bit but then decided to see Thomas. Cam commented on how cold the room was, the colourful blanket covering Tom and then decided he would improve the room for Tom. Cam and Tom had been given a tonne of Ben 10 action figures for Christmas just two weeks before. Cameron spent about 5-10 minutes carefully arranging them around the room and also on Tom's pillow. He looked up ready with justifications as to why each one had been placed where and the symmetry of size and shape in his grand design. "Looks awesome Cam, Thomas would love this". He smiled and it was so sweet to see him take such care and pride with looking after his brother one more time. Cameron didn't visit Thomas much after that – he spent time offering to help the office ladies at the hospice, playing with the other children staying there and showing me every new discovery he had made: the musical instruments in the garden, the chalk drawing he had done on the pathway, the small room under the fort where he could hide.

The staff at Hummingbird House were incredible. They took care of our meals, our laundry, helped us making arrangements and also gave us time alone. Friends and family could visit but they were also willing to keep the callers at bay if we needed. Nothing was too much trouble. The nurses suggested some things we could do that had helped other families in the past. We had someone come in to create casts of Tom's hands and ours. I have a casting of Tom's and my hands in our favourite hold: Big hand, little hand. I have Tom's fingerprint on a silver pendant that I keep in his memory box. It had been a few days before I talked with Dr Steve about whether or not he wanted posthumous access to Tom's tumour for research and tumour banking. He said that the timeframe for that had passed. It may or may not have been valuable to the research, but I wasn't too upset about that. Perhaps this was selfish in the grand scheme, but I needed the time to sit with my Tom, I needed to get my fill, to say every word I needed to say. It was a cathartic time that I know helped me very much in the time that was to come.

The most valuable experience suggested to us was to hold a Candlelit vigil for Tom. On the rooftop terrace we took turns reading to Thomas as the sun set on a Wednesday evening. Cameron took great delight in reading a book about dinosaur poop to Thomas. He read to all of us as well and shared the pictures with constant giggles at the irreverence of it all. We moved our observance to the garden to watch the stars come out. There were fairy lights all around and we blew bubbles standing around Tom lying on his bed. Tom was covered in a colourful blanket that had been donated to us during our months in hospital. My three sisters, my mum and I all laid roses around Thomas – they were the colour of a sunset with hints of orange and yellow and red. Cameron and Lula placed stalks of baby's breath. Then the night fell dark and it was time to say our last goodbyes. We surrounded Tom and sang songs, cried over him and kissed his perfect forehead. I didn't think I would be so calm, but it was a beautiful evening to spend with my family and my son and I had found a trace of peace.

Keeping the tradition of alternating our favourite songs, in that garden, I played songs for him and songs for me that night. Tom knew my favourites well and used to sing along with me. Mine were always the slow ballads and his were exclusively upbeat so we had a good balance. That night I played song called **"Shine a Light"** by Armon Jay. The verses are sung almost in a whisper and to me sounds as if the singer might fall apart if he were to sing any other way. His words plead for light, for reprieve, for a return of what he'd lost. This song speaks very clearly of my functionality, or lack thereof and my grief in that week. I recalled the words that Karen had said to me – this was the worst thing that I was going to have to go through, but I would survive it. I just needed to find some light… and that night I did.

There is only one other thing that I reflect on when I think about Tom's death. He was peacefully asleep, warm in a soft bed surrounded by his family. He was free from pain and he'd had a chance to come to terms with what was happening in his own way. There was no violent shock, there was no terror, pain or drawn out suffering. We had made memories and had a chance to prepare as a family. I had been grieving for months and I know it will never stop. But I had 13 months from the date of his first diagnosis until the day he died on the 9th January, 2019. I'm cheered to have spent those months working with Tom, caring for him and watching his courage shine time and time again. Better that than to be dealt with an immediate loss. I can't imagine the additional impact of losing a child in an instant or through sudden circumstances. I feel there would be an extra weight on those parents, and I am so very sorry for anyone that has, or will, endure that. While it doesn't diminish how intense my pain is at losing my Thomas, my seven-year-old boy, I know that he was at peace when he passed and as a mum, as his mum, I will always be grateful for that.

Practical Advice:

- A Children's Hospice is not actually a 'sad place'. It's colourful and full of light, specifically designed to accommodate children with life-limiting conditions and provide for end-of-life care. It is not the same as a hospital.

- Cameron found joy in and around the hospice, with other kids, new surroundings and the ease of moving between his family members.

- The hospice is a central place to arrange for meetings in the lead up to the funeral service.

- Delegate the 'telling' of everyone – get a relative, a friend and hand them your phone.

- If you post an announcement on Facebook, be clear about wanting space and that you aren't going to answer the phone.

- Watching your child die is a bloody terrible thing and the worst possible thing you can imagine you will go through. But you get one shot at giving your child a good death and if you have the power to do that, it might bring you solace.

- <u>Supporters:</u> Be 'They who are present' and remember to bring a smile and a hug along with your tears and tissues.

- <u>Co-Parents:</u> The best decision we made was for Tom to spend his last day in the hospice. The facility allowed all of us to be close to Tom and also space to grieve separately.

Chapter 10

A Superhero Takes Flight

A Farewell

One day at the local pool Owen and Cam had gone over to the slides and left Thomas and me in the rehabilitation pool. I asked Tom what he thought of the conversation we'd had about his egg coming back and it being too strong to fight this time. He said to me again, "That I'm going to die when I'm a kid?" I said yes. He just kept looking at me but didn't say anything. I said to him, "I can tell you how I feel about it. I'm so sad Thomas. I have never been so sad, and I cry all the time. I am so upset that you have to go to heaven. I try not to cry in front of you, but you know it's ok to be sad". Tom actually looked surprised when I said this. Like he didn't realise how upset I would be. I had been trying to hold myself together so as not to add to his pain or fear.

I followed up with, "But remember honey, our warning time means we can do whatever you want". He replied, "I can tell people to do whatever I want?" I laughed and said, "Well not exactly. I mean, you could insist that everyone wears…pink to your funeral if you want to but mostly I mean we get to plan any adventure you want". He thought for a moment and said, "Not pink mum, Superhero shirts". I agreed this was a great idea. "Superhero shirts and transformer bottoms," he continued. I said, "Well that might be trickier, but we can keep thinking about plans for that later if you want". I asked again about an adventure, but he was finished talking about it all. He changed the subject and swam over to the rails to pull himself along the wall. I thought to myself, in a few days I'll try again.

When we were making our plans and deciding on the details of Tom's service, this conversation was in the back of my mind. I thought of the myriad of superhero t-shirts in his cupboard and that's where it took us – Tom was my hero; he was a hero to so many and so that was our theme. I had been to funerals of children before and they will always be the most heart-wrenching to witness. My main remembrance of these events is shock, tragedy and a pervasive sense of heaviness. These children had been taken suddenly, by way of accident – not illness. None of them had their chance to consider their mortality, let alone their funeral. I used the words funeral even though on the day we called it a "Celebration of Life". At no time did I feel like celebrating. At the same time, I didn't want the dark heaviness of the traditional funeral to be how Thomas was remembered on that day. Quite the contradiction really, but in the same way, so is the attempt to match the concept of youth with death. So here I was. The week before, but particularly the evening before, I had spent my time with Tom. I had been as selfish as I wanted with my Tom. I said so much of everything that I had needed to say to him, to myself, to the universe. I cried over him, I sang to him, I read to him, I held him. That was my opportunity. That evening was for me. The service or 'celebration' was for Thomas and everyone else who knew him. That was my mindset on the day as well – this needs to be a celebration of Tom. Everyone, see how amazing my son is!!!

A SUPERHERO TAKES FLIGHT

We engaged a lovely woman, another Karen, from Compassionate Funerals, to help us organise the service. She was just what we needed in a funeral director and she was the celebrant as well. Karen asked us questions about Thomas, she wanted to know him. Karen was looking for the best ways to authentically present him on this day. While allowing us time to make decisions, I also felt that everything that had to be organised was in good hands. There were timelines to meet and we met them. There were decisions to make and we made them, but for some reason I didn't feel rushed. In amongst the planning, I could go and sit with Tom. Karen also had the important position of ensuring both parents were able to feel comfortable with the plans made. I can't imagine that dealing with split families is an easy thing to do, especially during such a time of grief and stress.

From making announcements, considering logistics and sorting out relevant funding from charities, Karen was our go-to during that week. She told me one day that people react differently to that week between the day when their loved one leaves and the day of their funeral. Some go into an organisational frenzy; some can't commit to decisions at all. Some are heavily influenced by extended family, some do it on their own. I had been crying for months by this time and still in that week I would often break down in my moments alone. Crying every night going to bed, and every morning waking up. Through the day, when it came to arranging the service, somehow I could focus and I wasn't overcome with distress. Perhaps my mindset was still in mum-mode of 'what can I do for Thomas? I need to do this for my Tom'.

The brief for Tom's celebration was colour and light. Superhero shirts, vibrant balloons, banners and boards covered with enormous images of Thomas. These banners showed Tom as a baby, a toddler, a brother, a friend and a son. People saw him at the beach, in the park, at our wedding, at his school. There were pictures of Tom well and pictures of Thomas in hospital. With a full head of hair and in others, he was completely bald. He was running in some and smiling from his wheelchair in others.

On the Wednesday night, before we brought Thomas up to the rooftop we went in to get him ready to leave his room at Hummingbird House and eventually go to the funeral home. Karen walked us through changing him into his Spiderman pyjamas. I talked to Tom as if we were getting dressed on any regular day. My words were soft and apologetic as I pulled his hands through his sleeve and moved him around. My heart was in full heart-pinch the whole time and I kept thinking – this is my last time. I'd dressed him countless times from the first time on the maternity ward to this cold room in a children's hospice. This was my last time and I thought I couldn't bear it.

Tom's casket was beautiful. Karen found someone who could design anything you wanted on a coffin. We asked for it to be covered in Tom's favourite heroes. The Teen Titans, Ben 10, the Transformers: Optimus Prime and Bumblebee, Spiderman and we even managed to get the Lego face on one end. All on a background of a deep, purplish-blue – and it was perfect. Cameron loved the coffin and was adamant that Thomas would have been so excited to see it. As I've already mentioned, Tom had a great love of soft blankets and delighted in cuddling up in one. We took his favourite blanket in navy blue in a material plusher than velvet, and lined the casket before we lay him down. It was so big, we could wrap him up and he looked cosy and peaceful, surrounded by favourite toys – a long-limbed rabbit from his sister and the police dog given to him at the station. One to comfort, one to protect. Karen's assistants then covered Thomas with the lid, adorned with a massive image of Spiderman in full flight. That was the last time I saw my boy.

I still remember the day of the service very clearly. It was hot – January in Queensland, Australia is notoriously hot, humid and sweaty. Owen and I arrived early to set up banners and position balloons and tables, etc. Sharon and her husband Aaron, Ben and Danielle were also on hand to arrange. Thankfully there was glorious air conditioning already cooling the room and so it was bearable inside. I wanted to be there when Thomas arrived. The police from the Holland Park Station had offered to provide Thomas with a police escort and an honour guard. I watched them arrive, complete with "Punch", the beautiful German shepherd standing at the ready. Toby, the driver from Compassionate Funerals, had taken the time to attach an Iron Man toy and a Spiderman to the roof and hood of the hearse. The blokes had also organised to make formal ties out of superhero fabric. I had struggled with what I would wear but had a last-minute revelation that I could have a dress made. The same woman who made my wedding dress in just two weeks managed to design and deliver a custom-made dress in Wonder Woman comic strip fabric.

After I was happy that Thomas had been safely placed at the top of the room, I left to find a room to change. Before I put on my makeup, I read out my speech to Owen for one final practice. I had only written it the night before and had still not made it to the end without sobbing. I was metres away from where Tom's service would be. The time was coming close and this time I managed to get through it. Owen was trying so hard to focus but he was in tears fairly early on. "It's perfect Trish," he said. So, I felt ready. I drank some water and started to apply layers of makeup in an attempt to cover the bags under my eyes and the puff above them. As I saw myself squinting in the mirror, I recalled a conversation I had with my Aunty Sam on the day of my grandmother's funeral.

My grandmother passed away two decades ago, and she and I didn't really get on very well. Of course my mother and her sisters were upset, and this was really the first death in the family that I had experienced as an adult. My Aunty Sam came out to the living room ready to leave with us. She had been crying the night before and I knew she would cry again that day. I asked her: "Why are you wearing eye makeup? Won't it just get ruined?" I was no expert on makeup, but I knew that mascara and eyeliner weren't going to handle the flood. She responded, "Well, I want to look nice for her". I reflect back on how rude it was to ask her that but at the time I thought I was being helpful. This conversation came back to me as I carefully ran my eyeliner across my lid and stroked fresh mascara onto my lashes. Today was for Tom and I wanted to look nice for him.

Once I was ready, Owen and I headed up to the marquee at Victoria Park. We knew a lot of people would come so Karen had found us a space to accommodate approximately 500 seats. Even that wasn't enough with rows of attendees standing at the back. I thought it best to visit the ladies room before going in and I remember thinking, I hope there's no one in there that I know. As soon as I thought that I *knew* that I was going to see someone I knew in there. What was I going to say? I'm in a small room, washing my hands and two lovely women I knew are standing on either side of me. I imagine they didn't know what to say either. I break the ice with, "Ha, nervous wee". I felt one of them touch me gently, the other was looking at me in the mirror. I don't remember anything else. I just left. Owen walked me to the front of the room, full of people, of balloons, of colour and at the head of the aisle I saw Tom's casket. Then I dropped my head and looked at the floor until I got to my seat.

I found it much easier on the day of his service when looking at Tom's coffin. A colourful casket, covered in Superhero images, smaller than an adults' but long enough for my tall, skinny boy. We placed our symbols on the casket: a scarf from me, a superman-style pool floatie from Owen and Lego from Cam to name a few. We lit his candle and Tom's godfather gave a blessing. Our celebrant Karen formally started the service with an explanation of the significance of the superhero images. Transformers were a favourite toy for both boys and I used that as a theme in my 'Letter to Tom'. A standard eulogy for an adult is an account of one's life: when and where they were born, schooling, work, relationships, interests, etc. Thomas had died 11 days before his 8th birthday. I was the keeper of his life story to date but for me writing my letter to Thomas was about describing how amazing he was. There were people there that might have only known Tom through his parents, without having actually spent time with this beautiful boy. There were hospital staff there that only knew Thomas post-surgery and perhaps weren't aware of the boy he had been before. My letter to Tom was built around the concept of transformation and I repeated a mantra throughout: "I held you, I whispered to you, I sang to you". This letter was entitled, Every Version of You. Here are some excerpts of how I spoke about my Tom that day:

Excerpt A

Then you transformed into a young boy. It happened too fast. We both love to dance, to cuddle, and being cosy is one of our favourite feelings – you are just like me in so many ways. Such an affectionate and tactile boy - I love it when you stroke my face, grab me in a fierce hug or tell me you love me. We both feel the cold and when I wasn't watching you would get a hold of my soft scarves and blankets and cuddle up so tight, wear it like a hood or even make a simple bed fort by throwing it over your head. When you are sad, sick or a bit overwhelmed you stretch out your hand to me. "Big hand, Little hand" we say and then we interlock our fingers and squeeze. It is one of my favourite rituals with you.

Excerpt B

13 months ago, we found the egg. The egg in your head called cancer. The biggest fight of your life and I watched you transform yet again. Your surgery attacked the egg, but it sent you back to square one in so many ways. This last year I watched you re-find every neuro pathway back to every muscle. Step-by-step. You learned to move, to sit, to speak, to hold, to stand, to move your fingers, to swallow and you did all this with such grace and patience. In such a frustrating time, I saw your next version bring forward resilience, strength, courage and persistence. Amongst the battle of cancer treatments on top of brain injury you found a way to smile. To find joy in the confines of a hospital bed or a wheelchair. Don't get me wrong, your eyebrows could always express your discontent and you had your blow ups. But you didn't give up even when you wanted to. I saw a new version of my Tom arise from this struggle. You were transformed in my eyes and you became my hero. Our hero. Through it all, I held you, I whispered to you, I sang to you.

Excerpt C

These last 13 months, I have been your mum, your carer, your nurse, your pillow, your rehab therapist. I am now adrift and shattered to pieces. I am transformed, I am different. I will never be the same. How did my little boy manage it with such grace in the face of such adversity? It's all so messy in my head and in my heart. I am having a million feelings and thoughts at once and I sometimes think I will fly apart without you to anchor me. I'm devastated, proud, angry, overwhelmed, regretful, sorry, tired, but most of all, I guess I must be and I am…grateful. No amount of time would ever be enough, but I am grateful that I had almost eight years with you. That I had this time caring for you and saw what an amazing soul you are. That you showed me what patience and resilience really looks like. That you passed away in my arms,

A SUPERHERO TAKES FLIGHT

in peace, and free of pain and fear. That I get to share with all of these people today what an incredible person you are. For all of these things I am fortunate and I am thankful.

Tom's dad also wrote him a letter, as did Cameron. We helped guide Cam in writing his letter and decided to film him reading it so there wouldn't be any pressure on the day for him. He talked about how lucky he had been to have a best friend in Tom and so was never alone. Cam remembered his favourite things they did together and the fact that Thomas always chose the best presents. He said he would remember him in the places they visited, and he finished with a promise to look after their sister, their mum and dad. Cameron also had an important role on the day. He joined the pallbearers: Tom's father, step-father, godfather and close family friend. They had affixed a fifth handle at the end of the casket for Cameron to hold and when the time came he walked his brother out of the room. I watched him walking in front of me, staring at the back of his head. I was shaking like a leaf and crushing Danielle's hand as she walked me out of the room behind my two boys.

We engaged a company called Tasteful Transitions to collect and assemble some video collage type presentations of Tom. We had three altogether. The first looked at Thomas in his first six years of life: as a baby, a toddler, a beach lover, a student, a gorgeous carefree young boy. This video was entitled 'Our Tom'. Then we showed everyone the video depicting his last 13 months in hospital. His courage, his spirit and his resilience as he battled away in the face of so much. This video was called 'Our Hero' and the final video was kept for the end as a collection of solo portrait photos of Tom. The music accompanying these photos was mostly uplifting and energetic in style. Karen suggested to us there should be some chance for the audience to reflect. I chose the song **"Send Me The Moon"** to play for this section of the ceremony. Thomas and I used to listen to this song and it was a very true representation of what I was going through in his final days and in the week that followed. I would wish for the night so I could perhaps see him in my dreams. I had held it together for most of the service but when this song was played, I began to cry.

I had talked with Karen about my experiences at my dad's funeral approximately 18 months before. I had never been in the front row of a funeral before his and so it was a new experience to me then. I spoke at Dad's funeral and learned that the key rule to speaking and not becoming overwhelmed was to avoid looking at my sister, Felicity. I knew that I would just have to apply that to everyone and look over their heads. The other important lesson I learned that day was when the most pain hit me. As Dad's pallbearers carried his casket out of the church and to the hearse my mum, my sisters and I followed him first. I held on to whoever was holding onto me and the reality and the finality of it all came in a rush. I could hear my sister, Steph crying out. The people on either side of the aisle were a blur to me as tears trailed down my face and I guess I was walking on autopilot. Mum and Steph had decided they would follow Dad to the crematorium but the rest of us girls, me, Felicity and Josey, stayed behind. I remember watching the hearse move off and turning around to see crowds of people. All lined up to hug me and kiss me and give me words of comfort. That was confronting considering I had just had this momentous feeling of grief and emotion overwhelm me on that short walk out of the church.

I knew I couldn't have that on Tom's day. I knew that I would dread that moment from the instant the ceremony began. It would distract me from the actual happenings of the service, and I wouldn't get those moments back. I needed to remember everything that happened, to experience every moment properly. I was the holder of Tom's memories and this was a final one to catch. When I mentioned this concern to Karen, we made a plan to circumvent this. After the service, Owen and I would follow Thomas in the car to a green park about 10 minutes away from the venue. There I could spend time with Thomas, to cry, to breathe, to talk, to sit. Whatever I wanted. That way, perhaps that dose of reality would be easier to take knowing I had more time, that the walk wasn't the 'end'. As we watched the pallbearers put Tom's casket into the hearse, I saw the policemen and women stand to attention. As we drove off in procession, I saw "Punch" and his human on the side of the road. I found out later that as we passed the police dog, he broke into a run and followed the car for a short time. Tom would have loved that.

At the park, I sat next to Tom's casket on the back bumper of the hearse – how surreal is that? – and I felt peaceful. I saw a single droplet on the lid which was right near the image of Spiderman's head. It was someone's teardrop. I sat there talking away to Tom, while I rubbed at that droplet, spreading it around on the surface until the water was gone. Almost absentmindedly moving my finger in circles until it no longer left a trail. I tried to play some music, but my phone kept pinging me. Eventually I stood up. I had played every song and told him I loved him more than one million times over. I was ready to say goodbye. And my goodbye wasn't coloured with bawling and screaming to the skies. I had done that already. I didn't need to do that in a northside park on a Thursday afternoon. I said goodbye to my Bubba, told him I loved him, and I would be waiting for his visits. I kissed his coffin lid on Spiderman's forehead and waved to the driver.

When Owen and I returned to the marquee from our time at the park, we walked in to see crowds of people although many had already left. People were unsure if we would return and so headed back to their working day. I quickly found myself to be desperately hungry and very keen for a wine. I had been living with all of this tension and it was slowly draining out of me. As I moved around the room, every person I passed would stop me. In many cases, I hadn't seen a lot of these people in a long time. Some I hadn't even met. We all have our habits of interaction and I found the first thing almost every person said to me as they gave me a hug was, "How are you?" A very innocent and common inquiry for anyone you are worried about or haven't seen for a long time. Then realisation would dawn on their faces and one of two things would happen. Either they would immediately correct themselves and apologise for asking or they would stand there, feeling awkward but letting the question stand and hope for the best. In these brief dealings I had with so many people that day I realised that there would be times when I would need to make it ok for others when they were unsure how to talk to me. Indeed, there were some people who couldn't actually speak to me; every time they tried they would break down. Interestingly, these people were usually middle-aged men, some fathers, some not. The impact of Tom on these men really moved me.

That day I fully realised the impact of my son, his story and his death. Over 500 people attended Tom's service. This service was intended for adults only, so this was a pretty amazing turn out. I saw old friends and new, relatives, work colleagues, ex-students, Tom's primary school teachers, swimming and gym instructors, childcare workers from when he was a bub, hospital staff, people who had journeyed from out of town, supporters of supporters. The community had joined us and Tom in such force and that

really inspired me. In our announcements, we had asked people to come dressed to fit the superhero theme or if not that, to wear bright colours. I was so touched by the effort that everyone put into their attire and I recall standing at the microphone and seeing a sea of so many bright colours. I didn't fix my gaze on any faces, but it was a stunning sight and I hope Tom saw how awesome it all was.

I moved around the room and after chatting with most people I settled in to find my closest friends and amongst their faces, I drank wine and I found a way to smile. I hugged a lot of people that day. I heard many lovely things said to me about the service and about Thomas. We had made a deliberate decision to ask people not to bring their children to the ceremony. Perhaps it seemed weird that kids weren't invited to a child's funeral but (a) there wasn't room for an extra 100 or so children and (b) I needed that day to be calm, not made frantic by herds of little ones. So instead, we asked people to bring their children to a separate event ten days later. We called it our Children's Celebration Day for Thomas and had over 100 people enjoy the day. Friends offered to help with every little task to ensure we had shade, food and entertainment. We organised games, a Lego station, cupcake decorating and a colouring table. There was a bouncing castle, a balloon twister, a face painter and a sausage sizzle. A hot January day also called for a water bomb fight and a slip-n-slide. We played music, plastered up photos of Tom and asked kids to add their fingerprint leaf to new canvases marked out with trees. The whole she-bang! Families were sent home with CDs of Tom's favourite tunes and it was a wonderful day. My hope is that people will think of these days each summer and remember my beautiful boy, Thomas.

Practical Advice:

- Guessing the number of attendees and then finding an appropriate venue is the trickiest bit because funeral announcements need to go out quickly. Once this is done, there is less pressure in terms of decision-making.

- Don't be afraid to add some celebration into your service for your child. If a traditional service sits better with you, then by all means! But it is ok for you to make it exactly as you want it, to best reflect the memory of your son or daughter.

- I found that my moment alone with Thomas in the park following the service was really helpful for my state of mind, during the funeral and afterwards. This is something you can request if you think it will help.

- I had my friend Sharon standing off to the side as I read out my letter. She passed me water when I needed it and was ready to take over if my emotions were too much. If you don't think you can speak you have options: give the job to your celebrant, have someone at the ready to help you if you want to try, or even consider the option of videoing your speech before the day.

- If you have a friend or family member willing to help with slide shows of photos, don't be afraid to give them a job. I have done these for other people, but I really couldn't dedicate the time to this project in the week before the service. Delegate whatever you can.

- <u>Supporters:</u> Help with the service if you can offer to fulfil a role or just attend and witness their journey.

- <u>Co-Parents:</u> Instead of a single guest book, consider having lots of small pieces of card or paper that people can write on. Ours were in different shapes (stars, hearts, etc) and colours. Our funeral home offered to collect them and scan them so both families had a copy of the people who attended, their thoughts and well wishes.

- <u>Co-parents again:</u> Remember to compromise where you can in planning and decision making – each of your memories have an important place in the service but in the end it is about your child.

Chapter 11

No Such Thing

Immediate Grief – the First Three Months

They say you start grieving the moment you are told that your child is incurable – it's called anticipatory grief. I had been in this state for almost two months. Now, Tom was gone. No more organising to do, no more visits to the hospital, no more night-time cuddles. Anticipatory grief is a scratch compared to the amputation that is bereavement. There were a number of things that crystallised for me in the first few months of grieving for Thomas. A fair bit of it is explicitly described in the song **"No Such Thing"** by Sara Bareilles. I didn't want to feel better, happier. I wanted to soak in my pain. If I didn't feel his loss every minute, then that meant I didn't love him as much as I did. I still felt Thomas everywhere, but he was nowhere. For the first few weeks I was happy to just go along in a fuzzy numbness that would sporadically be interrupted by tears. I was surrounded by people but in a constant state of loneliness, for my little boy, my teammate. I know it seems ridiculous to listen to sad songs, music that is an immediate trigger to sorrow, but I needed the release again and again of sitting and crying. The experts say to make time to sit with your grief, lean into your grief, give your grief time and work through it. This song helped me do that because it validated every thought and feeling I was having – that I had no intention of ever 'getting over' this loss. There was no such thing.

I remember seeing a doctor, just a local GP who didn't really know me very well, but I was there to get some sleeping tablets. I wasn't sleeping. I wanted to sleep so I could dream about Tom. This was something I would clutch on to because I'd heard other people would dream about their loved ones, but Tom didn't visit me. I had also spent the last 13 months in a constant level of alertness for when Tom would wake in the night. Whether in hospital or at home, Tom would wake in the night or the early hours of the morning, so I stopped having any real deep sleep. Even when Thomas was at his dad's place, I would never fully relax into sleep because of this habit, this worry that I wouldn't hear him. In fact, I began to notice that at night I would start to have this background feeling of unease that wouldn't fade until the next day. I couldn't figure out what was causing it or how to fix it. I came to realise this always happened around the boys' bedtime. It was always after I had put Cam down for bed. I would start to worry. This feeling of disquiet was because I hadn't put Tom to bed. My body couldn't relax until I had put them both to bed. I had been doing this since I first became a mum. Putting two boys down for sleep, not one. So instead of putting Tom to bed, I would sit down and go through photos, hoping that this feeling would stop.

I told this doctor about my son's passing and that I would like something to help me sleep. She said something to me that I guess a lot of people say to the newly bereaved: "Time heals". Whether that is true or not, that was not something that I agreed with in the early stages, even now. The passing of time was devastating to me. I hated that time was passing. It didn't feel like healing. I didn't want more time to pass because it put more distance between me and the last time I held my boy, the last time I spoke with him or laughed at his crazy menu suggestions. I wanted to freeze time and settle into a space where he and I were still together. When he was warm and cheeky and needed a cuddle. So the concept of 'time' could get stuffed.

My very good friend, Emma, had twin boys a few years after I had mine. I know Emma is a very capable mum, but she would often come to me asking for advice about raising twins, raising boys, etc. She would ask, "When your boys were two did they ever…?" Or, "How old were your boys when…?" Now, I had planned on keeping a journal as a new mum. I seriously thought I would. But, for some reason I was a little busy during the day managing the twins and up at night so surprise, surprise…!!!…I absolutely did not keep a journal. I tried so hard to recall specifics for Emma and to do my best advising her on ways that might help or to set her mind at ease. My memories had faded though, or perhaps I had blocked some of it out, who knows? I was thinking to myself: I have memories of when the boys were little, but only some of them stick. I remember one particular day in the park giggling on a blanket, another day I found Thomas eating dog vomit on the living room carpet, and a time I found both boys covered from head to toe smeared in Vegemite on the couch. I have some photos and videos that remind me of other times, and it floods back. Even memories I have of my own life. I remember a day in grade two as a gangly seven-year-old girl, when I conquered every post in the row of jump frog in the playground. I cannot recall any other day in that year. This is the way it is. Our mind doesn't retain it all, and sometimes we can't pick what will stay and what we will lose.

This brings me to the next issue I had in my initial stages of grief: the fear of forgetting. I had rising levels of anxiety that I would forget things. Forget memories of Tom, of anecdotes, of things he loved to do, eccentricities that were just Tom. I was the keeper of Thomas' history. I knew him better than anyone. How he moved in my belly, how he ran with straight arms, how he loved bath time and getting the most water onto the floor. Our bedtime ritual, one I also practiced with Cam, was the 'Dreamcatcher'. I used to pull the bad dreams from his head and replace them with good dreams that I could catch from the air. I'd run my fingers through his fine hair searching for a 'bad dream'. I'd stop suddenly and say, "Oh! I found one!" Then I'd pretend to drag that bad dream to the edge of his head and miraculously pull it out with my fingers. I would throw it away and go looking again.

After removing about three, I went about replacing them with happy dreams. I'd look around the room, at the space just above his bed, my eyes darting here and there. I'd reach across quickly and say, "Got one! Oh, Tom it's a great dream". As I rubbed my fingers in a circle in his hair, I'd tell him all about this particular dream. "This one has a playground with the tallest slide you've ever seen." Or it would be about winning the top prize or visiting the most beautiful beach on the sunniest day. Then I would give his head a final little press and say, "Ok, it's in!" How many times I wished I had that magic to save my son. To draw his tumour out of his head with just my fingers. No scalpel, no anaesthetic, no scars, no fuss. I'd dream of pulling it out slowly and carefully almost like in a cartoon and then once it was out, tossing it like a basketball into the rubbish bin.

In the first few months, my fear of forgetting things started to really impact my thoughts and my ability to relax. This also bled into my fear of *others* forgetting. When people talk to me about Tom, when they say they remember him – I get immediately teary and thank them. Georgia, Tom's speechie in 8A, told me she thinks of Tom every time she hears Ed Sheeran. Isabella, one of Tom's teachers at the hospital is reminded of Tom whenever she hears the song **"Thunder"**. One of our social workers Alana tells me she is reminded of Tom whenever she sees the three-wheeler bikes in the corridors of level six. I gave a photo of Tom to each of his therapists and they all say they have his photo on their desk. At the time of writing this book, he hasn't even been gone a year and so I wonder if years down the track I'll still be impressing on people the need to remember him. His face, his strength, anything about him. The most amazing feeling comes when people from the hospital say how fondly they remember Thomas. That they think of him often and he still inspires them. They see so many children, some get better, some pass away. For some reason it is still so important to me that everyone hold his memory. That he cannot be forgotten.

I know that life moves on for other people – I think of all the people in my life that I have farewelled. Depending on the person, their place in my life before they died – whether daily or otherwise – my observance of them is not constant or even prevalent in some cases. I know that the people who will think of him every day is confined to me and a select group. At this point in my grief I wanted to fixate on maintaining his presence in my conversations, my actions, my future…but I know that this is not the path most take – at least in a public setting. It makes others feel uncomfortable perhaps if you are still focused on your loss after a period of time has passed. I love it when people feel comfortable enough to mention Thomas. I will take any opportunity to talk about him, to remember him. The more often we do, the more present he is in my life.

There is also a surrealism to my experience of initially grieving for Tom. At first I could pretend. Pretend that Tom's room was empty because he was just at his dad's that night. I could pretend for a moment when Cam ran ahead that it was Thomas running ahead. I could tell myself that it had never happened. That was how I coped for a little time, but it didn't last. It couldn't. As Cam grows up he will no longer resemble his seven-year old brother. Cam will be the picture of what Tom would have looked like as an adult. But it won't be him. I think Owen believed that I must have developed a true addiction to social media, as I constantly looked down at my phone. It wasn't that. I don't mind a bit of Facebook for a cheap meme giggle or a glassy-eyed scroll, but I was usually working through my gallery of photos. There were times that I had an intense need to hear his voice or see his face. It would settle the heart pinch that would randomly take my breath away. It would calm me down for a moment when the reality of Tom's death would hit me again and again. Sometimes, though, it would start me off on a big cathartic crying session. There were times I just needed that. In the early days if too many hours had passed between my chance to have a cry or remember Tom, I would feel this rising anxiety. I couldn't quite identify the reason for this build up when it was happening, but I knew where it came from after I had some time with Tom's photos and memories. So, I learned to let it happen. I would excuse myself, find a place to be alone and just let it fall out of me.

When I would find myself alone was usually a time that grief would visit. Mostly, in the car or the shower. I'm sure I looked fairly crazy, driving along on my way home from the shops weeping quietly or wailing like a banshee at the wheel. I tried to be safe and if it got too bad, I'd pull over. Triggers would happen so many times in a day. These were things like certain music, seeing other children and babies, anything twin-related, seeing kids sucking their thumb, even wheelchairs and Maxi-Taxis …my grief could be all pervasive some days and others I would have some reprieve. I was constantly tired from lack of sleep but from something else also. I had never needed more than about six hours sleep and had managed quite a busy life in the past. I didn't understand why I didn't have the energy to accomplish almost anything anymore. My psychologist told me, "grief is heavy Trish. You are carrying around this weight and it will drain you, your energy, your resilience. That's completely normal. Give yourself a break". There were times that I just needed to engage in mind-numbing activities to give myself a break from my reality. Working on puzzles, playing little games on the iPad, watching trashy shows on Netflix. Even trying to have naps to catch up when the night wouldn't let me sleep.

You also notice when it's all very fresh and raw, this grief that is in the back of your every thought and interaction, something I call 'First and Lasts'. I was hit by a realisation every time I did something for the *first* time since Tom had passed and then by the memory of the *last* time we did that together. This truly sucks! I vividly remember the first time I drove towards the city. I wasn't going to the hospital, but it was the same route for 70% of the way. It was the same time of day when Thomas and I would be on our way to our rehabilitation sessions. It was the same road and I was in the same car, all by myself. My rear-view mirror was in the same position – angled so I could see Tom's car seat. This day was the first time he wasn't in the mirror dancing to our songs or calling out, "Spotto!" Instead there was an empty seat and a heart pinch seized my chest.

Cam's swimming lesson had been moved to an afternoon when his dad would have him and so I hadn't done the swimming lesson thing in over a year. A day came when Cameron was with me for that day and I took him to his lesson. The first time I did this, I remembered the last time. That last time was December 9th 2017. The day Tom was diagnosed with a brain tumour. The day I saw him run to the outside toilets and I felt his cold hands against my cheeks to cool me down. The last day we ever walked from the pool to the car, holding hands. That 'first and last' hit me so hard I cried for the entire half hour lesson. Sat there, on a bench by the edge of the indoor pool, surrounded by parents and children everywhere, I let the tears fall and drench my t-shirt. That 'first and last' was truly awful.

These kept coming, particularly as they were things that still had to happen with Cameron. Haircuts, going to the bakery as we used to, visiting the dentist, going to the beach or walking down to Cleveland Point by the bay. After the first visit to the park or the beach, as I walked along seeing Owen and Cam up ahead, I would feel the beginnings of joy trying to make their way in. I would intentionally quash it. It was not ok to feel joy! How could I feel joy when Thomas wasn't here? I wouldn't let myself smile at the sunset or laugh at Cam's antics when this constant mantra of *'Thomas is dead'* played in the back of my mind. I started to feel guilt at even the thought of letting happiness enter my days. I felt guilt for everything. Every time I had been cross with Thomas in the past. Every time Tom endured another shitty thing at the hospital, and I told him it had to happen. Mother's guilt, wife guilt, personal guilt – guilt came at me from every corner. What a terrible mother I must be to have lost my son! I had failed my little boy, I had broken my million promises that everything would be okay. None of this was rational and deep down perhaps I knew that. It didn't change how I felt though and I felt it was a just punishment to carry this burden. That I deserved to feel this culpable and wretched. I second guessed everything I had done, every decision I had made, every word I had said. I was going crazy with it all. None of it made sense and my family would insist that there was no need to feel this way. Eventually, I realised that at some point I would have to make peace with all of my perceived mistakes and regrets or I wouldn't cope. I needed to find ways to cope for myself and for Cameron.

Tom's service was on the 17th January 2019 and it was the boys' birthday just three days later. I know I will always struggle with January. We worked hard to ensure Cam's birthday was celebrated and some much-needed attention could be sent his way. That night after he had eaten cake and played with mates, I settled him down and wished him a happy 8th birthday once more. I told him I was so proud of him and what a wonderful boy he was growing up to be. Then I went outside to the back patio. I had decided that I wanted to start a jigsaw puzzle. It was something Thomas and I had loved while he was in hospital and I thought this would be a nice tradition on the holidays. My friend Danielle had bought me one of a panda a few months before. I went to look for it but couldn't find it anywhere. The more I looked, the more frustrated I became. I kept thinking, each drawer and cupboard were so disorganised, we still had washing to put away, there was unopened mail on the counter. I became more and more upset by any mess everywhere I looked. I was in this storm of guilt about being a terrible mother with such a messy house and so I thought the only way I could fix this was to clean and tidy the house until it sparkled. Poor Owen looked on desperate to help me, insisting that I was a perfectly wonderful mum, but I wouldn't be swayed. I was in a frenzy of guilt and pain. So I spent the next hour tidying, room by room until...

I came across the jigsaw puzzle. I stopped then and took it outside to sit on the back patio. I started to cry, heaving with feelings of helplessness and profound misery. Eventually I took out a notebook and wrote another letter to Thomas. I sat there with a glass of wine, a candle flickering on the table and looking up at a very full moon as I wrote it all down and had a big cry. I was too wrecked to be starting the puzzle now so I fell into bed like a puddle. I admit that I am dreading next January and so will be more prepared. I will make conscious plans to get me through those days – his anniversary and his birthday and the eleven days in between. While each January will be charged with loss and heartache this will be counter-balanced as I watch Cameron celebrate each new birthday and start each new school year. Owen, Cam and I will spend time at Coolum Beach as we used to do each summer holiday. Perhaps I will find joy in this dreaded month one day. Perhaps.

My house is full of things that remind me of Thomas. Hummingbird House gifted us a Memory Box which is just beautiful. It came packed with thoughtful items such as a candle, a Christmas bauble, a journal and many more items of kindness. I used to add important reminders of Tom to the Memory Box but realised pretty quickly that I would need a bigger box. In our clean up, I struggled to throw away anything that even had Tom's name on it, let alone favourite books, toys and clothes. I have the box, but I also have a chest of memories that I keep. In there I can find the clothes Thomas wore to our wedding, his favourite toys, drawings, his cap from the police station. I even made a point of keeping some of the paraphernalia from the hospital to remember the final year of his life. A very important year to remember for me and so there is a collection of things like a syringe, a spit towel, the tape for his nasogastric tube, and the like. Apart from things that were his, we also had mountains of supplies from the hospital, in particular hundreds of nappies and boxes upon boxes of his feed formula. These were donated back to the hospice and I took leftover meds to the hospital pharmacy.

I decided during the first three months after Tom had died that I would write this book. That's a big deal because I had real trouble making even little, simple decisions – I had little concentration and limited interest or capacity to form an opinion. I figured this book would achieve a few things. First, I would have something tangible to hold in my hands of Tom's battle. It was a way I could never forget. As soon as I started writing, my fears surrounding this element of grief subsided. I guess to a certain extent it is a little self-indulgent in that respect, but it has helped. It also gave me a chance to become really clear about what happened. When you are in the middle of it all, you don't always know what questions to ask or what information you need. So I reconnected with the hospital staff, Dr Steve and Karen from the Pal Team and clarified my understanding of the small room conversations in a way that perhaps I could process a little better without the shock fogging my comprehension. In a meeting with Dr Steve I shared with him a dream I had of him. The dream went like this:

I was standing on the lawn space across the road from the hospital and in my arms, I held a baby (please note, I was not pregnant or trying to have a baby). All of a sudden Dr Steve came out from a nearby building to say, "Hi!" He asked if he could hold the baby and I agreed. Then a nurse came out to ask me some medical questions about my bub and when I turned around, Dr Steve was gone. So was my baby. I walked inside the nearby building and saw Dr Steve by the reception desk about to go through the doors leading further into the building. I called out, "Dr Steve, can I please have my baby back?" Dr Steve looked up at me with his 'small room face' – the one with the furrowed brow and the tight, frowning mouth, and then he was gone.

I realised the very explicit message of the dream was that Dr Steve had stolen my child. That deep down I blamed him for the loss of Thomas. That he was the face of the cancer that had taken Tom from me. I assured him that I don't blame him, I don't have anger towards him and that I feel we were very lucky to have had him in our corner, working hard to help get us through the whole thing to a point of recovery and remission. I asked him about his experiences with parents facing a future filled with oncology treatment and in some cases, a terminal diagnosis. A range of reactions from anger to a numb disbelief, to hysterical outcry. I know that the whole thing felt insurmountable but sometimes all I could hold onto was the hope that Dr Steve would give me. The hope that the therapists, the social workers, the doctors and the nurses would give us. We all gave it our best shot, no one more than Thomas, but we were fighting a battle that just couldn't be won.

I read a book called 'Any Ordinary Day' by Leigh Sales, an Australian journalist. This book investigates the impact of tragedy, loss and grief. How people are blindsided by catastrophic events and how they survive. Sales described an interview with the sole survivor of the Thredbo landslide, Stuart Diver, who talked about everyone having a set of core beliefs that are smashed apart when tragedy strikes. In the aftermath some of these beliefs are pieced back together, some are destroyed, and some are replaced. She found that those that best cope with loss and grief find ways to resettle or adjust their beliefs, their *schemas* about how to understand the world. Holding on to blame, whether it is directed at oneself, at doctors or a perpetrator is detrimental to the healing process, but it is an understandable reaction. I don't have anything to blame except some hideous disease that the world is working hard to defeat. We just didn't get there in time when it came to Tom or the millions around the world who have fallen to its curse.

So beyond the loneliness, the fear of forgetting, the guilt, the triggers and the millions of tissues I've ruined along the way, I remind myself of these few things in an attempt to cope:

BIG HAND, LITTLE HAND

- Tom lived a happy life for the seven years he was with us and was granted a peaceful and pain-free death.
- I have his every memory and have the opportunity and the determination to keep his memory alive.
- Losing Thomas wasn't anyone's fault.
- I love him and always will, even with a broken heart.

I found this quote which really hit home to me about grief:

Grief, I've learned, is really just love.
It's all the love you want to give but can't.
All that unspent love gathers up in the corners of your eyes,
the lump in your throat, and in that hollow of your chest.
Grief is just love with no place to go.

Jamie Anderson

Practical Advice:

- If you don't have to go back to work straight away, don't go. Give yourself some time to just sit. While keeping busy might feel like it's the right thing, your grief will still build up and your energy levels might not cope with doing everything at once.

- I found myself crying in public. I stopped caring what it looked like to other people. It happens and it's ok.

- If you are worried about forgetting things – write them down. Or if you aren't keen on writing, get a cheap recording device and talk out your memories. It'll be worth it one day even if it hurts at the time.

- Let the people around you know it's ok to talk about your child if you want to talk about them. Some people are worried they will make it worse. They don't know that it might be helpful.

- Whatever you're feeling is normal. Normal for you. No one can judge – grief is different for everyone.

- You don't have to hide, give away or throw out their things. Hold onto them as long as you want to. I spend time with Tom's photos, toys, drawings, and anything else. I'll get my fill and one day if I am ready, I will let these items go. Or I won't. And that's ok.

- Talking to a counsellor or psychologist has been very important to me. Sometimes a sounding board, sometimes a voice to reframe situations in your mind and sometimes with strategies to cope.

- <u>Supporters:</u> Keep checking on them after a few weeks, it doesn't go away. Invite them on a walk or for a coffee or turn up with a bottle of wine. Whatever you know will work with your friend.

- <u>Supporters again:</u> Your friend may not know what they need or how to ask. Try leaving it open or try being specific. Ask their spouse or family members for suggestions of what you could do. I found it tricky to make decisions.

Chapter 12

A Table for Two

Not Moving on, Moving Forward

Two very kind women I met during all of this gave me some advice on grief. It can be deceiving. When it first hits, you are immediately surrounded by support. You are also swimming in a fancy hormone called *adrenocorticotropin hormone (ACTH)* that your body releases and is designed to protect you. It helps your body cope, keeps it functioning for this first shockwave. Apparently, people will feel another hit of profound grief approximately 4-6 weeks after their loss when these hormones start to fade from their system. Following that, I heard talk that acute grief can last up to two years. I remember saying rather sarcastically, "well great". There is a TED talk that a number of people had sent my way in those first few months and beyond. The speaker has experienced a fair amount of loss and grief in her life and she asserts that people don't move on from grief, they move forward with it. It doesn't go away. As a widow she still talked about her first husband – he continued to be a part of her family's lives. I hope this is how it will be for me and my family.

People ask me, "How is Cameron doing?" It's a tricky question to answer. To begin with he had some trouble settling back into school. It was a new school year, with a new teacher. He had just had over two months off school dealing with some very intense stuff: first a period of unexplained 'fun time' which also lacked structure or focused discipline. This was followed by learning his brother was going to die and then watching that happen ten days later. Bouncing between his parents in the week that followed and then experiencing the enormity of a funeral attended by over 500 people. After 4-6 weeks, Cam did start to find his way in school and a visit to his psychologist told us that his grief would not necessarily come out the way it would for us. It would take time, years even. He was less likely to talk about it in one hit but questions would come out of the blue, thoughts about Thomas might make it into his artwork or writing at school. Sometimes Cam will mention Tom's death to complete strangers. That's tricky for me and tricky for these poor people who tend to freeze in shock at such an abrupt disclosure. I imagine that Cam wants to talk about it but is still figuring out how.

At home I found that Cam found comfort in supporting me. He had always prided himself on giving the best back massages and any time I started to show signs of sadness, he'd be there rubbing my shoulders. If I was crying, he would ask if I was sad about Thomas. I would say yes, and we would talk about Tom, remember our favourite stories of him together. I didn't try to hide my grief from him. I think it was important to be honest with him about the way I was feeling and the emotions that surround losing someone you love. That it's ok to cry. Cam sometimes holds out his hand and says "big hand, little hand" and at night will kiss me twice and say "that one's from Thomas". In the months further down the track, Cam has started to need more of my attention and constant reassurances. He will tell me he loves me repeatedly sometimes 20-30 times a day.

I know he worries. There are times when his level of apologetic outpouring is extreme. For a simple, "Honey, I've asked you three times to get in the shower, come on let's go," his response will be next level contrition where he might actually get quite upset. He once said, "Mum I have to be a perfect son, cause I'm all you have left". That's a lot of pressure for a little boy and so I try to help him understand. I say, "I'm going to give instructions, that's never going to change, and it doesn't mean that I am cross, or that you have to get upset if I have to repeat myself. It's a mum's job to help you remember how things are done. It's not about being perfect Bub." It's the best I can think of and apart from helping him through a psychologist and keeping lines of communication open, all I can do is my best. To be patient with attention-seeking behaviour and try to ease his insecurities around his worth. Cameron astounds me in so many ways though. One of my favourite things he said to me recently was, "Mum, I'm going to make sure that everyone knows about Tom – through the generations! I'll tell all of his stories to my kids and they'll tell their kids, and everyone will know him even though he's gone". How beautiful is that – how fortunate am I!

I have focused energy into finding ways to keep Tom's memory alive and one way is through legacy. Legacy is about sharing something that you had. More traditionally it might be about a possession but in the context of Tom's legacy, it is what I have witnessed, what I have come to know, insights (for want of a better word) that I have gained and what I have learned in this process. Legacy is passing on something valuable to people in the hope of making the world a better place. If I can pour my energy into a project dedicated to Tom's legacy, I feel he is still in my life. He is in my thoughts, my actions and my contributions. Thomas used to pick up rubbish walking from the car to his classroom. He'd say, "People shouldn't drop their rubbish, we have to look after the community". He'd been learning about the concept of 'community' in his lessons and was applying it to his life. What a precious poppet I thought at the time. I also said, "Just be careful Thomas. Some rubbish can be dangerous. Let me help you choose safe rubbish to collect and then what do we do? We wash our hands!" I loved that he showed concern for other people, for the world around him. That he wanted to help people and, in this spirit, I can find comfort in helping people also.

As a result, I do focus on legacy work in Tom's name. I commit to challenges and fundraisers. I raise awareness for different causes and hope to help bring positive change. In 2018, my family, friends and I raised over $10,000 for Redkite – a charity which helps families dealing with childhood cancer. In 2019, we raised over $14,000 for Hummingbird House. Next year we'll support a charity focused on brain cancer research. These projects bring me purpose and balance out the 'everyday' of life. Cam and Tom's gymnasium mounted a plaque in honour of Tom which is on display. I have written a book with the aim of helping others and also as a way of helping me. In these ways and more, Tom's spirit is still here.

When the dust settled in January, we started to work on a bit of the spring cleaning that had been on hold for over a year. We unpacked bags, cleared cupboards and started opening and filing mail that had grown into monstrous piles. I came across my Wonder Woman dress. The dress I had had made for Tom's service. I took it to the dry cleaner and when I brought it back home, I stood in front of my wardrobe. What to do with this dress? Would I ever wear this brightly coloured, retro-styled, comic strip dress again? It would always be the dress I had made for Tom's day. Did its origin make it a sad dress? A sad dress with flair…? Did this mean it should hang it at the back of my wardrobe and be left there for years and years? I was in a conundrum for a while there, standing in front of my open wardrobe. Holding this dress in its freshly laundered cover, I decided on a course of action. Each year I intend to have a new dress made. A dress with new superhero fabric fashioned in new designs but always in a retro 1950's style. Every year my collection will grow. Then my Wonder Woman dress will hang beside Spiderman, the Avengers and the Transformers to name a few. I will bring these beautiful dresses out for fancy work events and I will happily be that eccentric lady with the superhero style. And people will ask me about them. People who will not know this story. And I will say: my son Thomas loved these superheroes. And he is my hero. And so here we are.

The months that followed Tom's passing were particularly difficult and I am glad now to be through that early devastation. A lot of those feelings remain but something new started to come through. Rage. My psychologist was waiting for it. I didn't realise how profoundly angry I could get at the most inconsequential things. The fastest trigger of my wrath was witnessing pettiness. People with a lack of perspective. A thing that they can't possibly have to the extent that I think they should, because they haven't lost their son. When someone tells you they've had a really hard start to the year because they had to have a tooth pulled…umm…that's not a hard start to the year. When I spoke to a child in the park about his unsafe behaviour and the kid proceeded to give me a glare of contempt. While that child might think that I am 'the worst' because I've called them on their actions on the playground, I am thinking – well at least you get a chance to play. At least you aren't confined to a hospital bed or a wheelchair. At least you aren't DYING you entitled piece of work! See…rage. I keep it all in my head and maintain an expression of perfect neutrality, but I'm feeling it anyway.

This year, my friends and family signed up for a fundraising challenge which involved physical activity and exertion. These things are not my strong suit, but I was doing it to fundraise for Hummingbird House. We were Team Tom but there were lots of teams who had become involved. Teams wear team shirts and so there were lots of slogans to read on people's 'active wear'. I read one woman's shirt and my rage took me by surprise. It read, "Cancer picked the wrong chick. I beat cancer's ass!" Now, it is wonderful that this lady is cancer-free. That is great for her and she can be proud to still be here and climbing 5000 stairs with the rest of us. That phrase on her shirt really got to me though. Cancer picks people? Wrong people and right people? So if someone dies of this disease, do we assume cancer chose correctly, it chose the right person? Was my son the right person? 'I beat cancer's ass' also suggests (to me at least), that everyone who doesn't survive didn't have the strength, that they didn't fight as hard as you? Bullshit lady! My son was a bloody warrior. See…rage. I wanted to scream at her arrogance, I wanted to rip the shirt from her back. Of course, I did none of this and luckily this cancer survivor woman was far more athletic than myself (oh the irony) and could run well ahead of me. I didn't have to look at those words anymore, but the fury was still pretty wild in my heart. One day, I hope not to feel rage at these things. This is stuff I can't control and isn't intended to raise my blood pressure. But for now, it does.

The other thing that still frustrates me is how much time is wasted. I struggle to wait in queues, my irritation builds when dealing with incompetence and with people who talk absolute rubbish. I am learning to remove myself from those interactions as much as I can. I say, Trish, Thomas learned to be patient, he did it, you can too. But my patience is fairly limited. So is my resilience to be honest. Little things that I might have taken in my stride in the past have me close to tears some days. Exhaustion creeps up on me and the heaviness of grief even in the background of my every day, lurking in my subconscious…it takes a toll. I am disappointed by my brain and its apparent need to relive the bad stuff. Why can't a beautiful memory of Thomas and me flash into my mind when I am having dinner instead of an image of him in the Paediatric Intensive Care Unit. Tom's last moments haunt me when I would prefer our night-time chats and cuddles linger in my thoughts. Ugh! I feel my mind is being mean-spirited really, because just when you have a few moments of 'ok' it says, 'woah woah woah honey – back to sad please'. But you can't cry all of the time. Your body doesn't let you even if you want to - it gets so tired and you just can't. You might cry every day at different times, but not every minute.

A TABLE FOR TWO

I am adapting to my new normal I guess. Isn't that what they say? I had adapted to life changing around Tom's tumour and now it's time to adapt to his death. It is a rare day when my thoughts of Thomas are easy. I am presented with flashbacks of the most traumatic memories. They will shoot a sting into my eyes and clutch at my throat. They will pass though, and I do my best to shake it off and breathe. I look forward to a time when my days are full of the beautiful times with Tom flashing in and out. I've read a fair bit about experiences of other bereaved parents and there are some common themes that I identify with. The main one that comes through is this: As helpful as friends and family want to be, unless someone has lived through it, they can't understand. They can empathise, they can listen, they can cry along with you. And that is really important – I don't know where I would be without my friends. But really it's a closed club for those parents who have been through it. A very sad club; no one wants to join but when membership is forced upon you, there is a sense of understanding, connection and relationship that is there just through this common experience. That's why there are groups I guess – for the bereaved, for the alcoholics, for anyone who is on their knees and looking for another survivor.

As the months have trudged past I have found ways that alleviate my grief to a certain extent. I feel a very strong sense of the importance of rituals and dates. My mum has continued the game of Spotto even though it isn't something that I do every time I am in the car. So when I drive her places and she calls out Spotto, I am reminded and I join in. She does this to keep Tom in our lives and I love it. Each spring the kumquat tree by our back gate becomes laden with fruit. For years, Cam, Tom and I have played the game of throwing these small orange balls as far as we could down the descending driveway towards the road. A good toss would make the road and hopefully be squished by passing cars for good measure. A great throw would make it to the lawn covering the nature strip across the roadway. We returned to this ritual in September of 2018 when Tom was finally home. Cam would collect kumquats for Tom and himself. Together they would throw them, Tom sitting in his wheelchair and Cam standing beside him at the top of our little hill. This game will be a ritual for us every spring and we will talk about Tom and how much he loved it.

Every month on the 9th day I post a memory I have of Thomas. I describe this memory, how it made Tom who he was and I accompany it with pictures. For example: Tom's love of dancing and singing, his love of the snuggle; there are lots to choose from. I've signposted this date each month since he died and I decided that I would follow this tradition of remembrance for this first year.

On our car trips or when we were stuck in a new hospital bed, Tom and I would sometimes reiterate our plans for our first dinner date together. Thomas had been thinking to himself about how much he loved Italian food and that one day he would be a cook in an Italian restaurant. And then, he declared that one day he would own it. But in the meantime, he and I planned to visit an Italian restaurant for dinner one night. I recorded one of these planning conversations once when he was up in the ward:

A TABLE FOR TWO

Me: "Where will we go for dinner?"
Tom: "Restaurant. Italian restaurant."

Me: "What will we order?"
Tom: "We'll have garlic bread, lasagne, pizza or spaghetti."

Me: "That sounds delicious! And what will you have to drink?"
Tom: "Anything. Anything but adult drinks because I'm just a kid."

Me: "So can I have an adult drink and maybe you can have a juice?"
Tom: "Of course."

Me: "That sounds nice. Can I dress up in a nice dress for our date?"
Tom: "Sure."

Me: "I can't wait to go on our date."
(Tom smiles.)

Tom: "And I'll even bring my lollies too."

Me: "Will that be a nice little sweet treat at the end? Or…do you know what the Italians call ice-cream? Gelato. Gelati. Should we have some ice-cream at the end as well?"
(Tom nods.)

Me: "And what flavours would you get?"
Tom: "Banana, blueberry or strawberry."

Me: "Do you know the ones that I would get? Mango and passionfruit…and maybe vanilla. I think we've made great decisions - I think we will be very, very full at the end."

(By this point, Tom was almost falling asleep sitting up.)

Me: "And then we can get some fresh air and wander down the street."

Tom: "A stroll."

Me "A stroll yeah, in the moonlight. It sounds delightful."
Tom: "And I'll even buy some flowers if I have any money."

Me: "I think you do have some money. Your money box is pretty full these days. That would be very kind."
(Tom is struggling to keep his eyes open even more now.)

Me: "Should we have a little rest or should we play a game?"
Tom: "Game."

Every month on the 9th day, we have a special dinner for Tom. It's usually Italian but sometimes we mix it up with Mexican to remember his adoration for nachos. We toast to Thomas and we talk about him, the things we did together, how much he would love the food. Thomas and I never made it to our Italian restaurant, our table for two. That used to sadden me but now I prefer to think about all of our coffee dates and pub lunches and scoffing down flavoured milk. There are too many things that we didn't do, and I can't keep listing them off in my head – that only brings regret and reminds me how unfair it all is. The ritual of the Italian dinner date is still a part of Tom and me. It's important to me…and so we go. Doesn't hurt that I love pasta.

I have a plan to intern Tom's ashes in a beautiful rose garden where many of my older relatives are. Dad, my Aunty Shan, Grandma, Poppy and the great-grandparents. I like the idea of them surrounding Thomas. Looking after him. I haven't chosen his spot yet and so for the moment Tom's ashes are in a beautiful sculpture-like urn on my bedside table. After his first anniversary, I will take him to the garden but for now, I need him close. When I was choosing the urn, I saw at the back of the catalogue there were jewellery options. Pendants that could hold a small amount of ashes. My choice was made as a result of this story:

Months before he passed, Thomas had started to say, "I heart you Mum". That whole emoji thing was reaching the boys and he'd heard it on a TV show I think. He'd say it sometimes as I turned out the lights and he'd say it in the car. He would work so hard to make the heart shape with his two hands to match his statement. His fingers still struggled to follow the requests his brain would send down, so it took a lot of concentration and patience. To get his thumbs to meet at the bottom and then for each of his fingers to curve around to meet at the top – completing the heart. I had decided that I would be looking for heart shapes that might have been sent my way by Tom – that's a thing if you didn't know. You look for signs.

To begin with, you look with a touch of desperation. It has to be where you wouldn't expect it. In the first week in particular I found hearts everywhere: I saw one on the wooden table over dinner in a pub. The condensation puddles of Owen's beer had formed a heart. I saw it in the clouds, I saw it in leaves. When your mind is constantly on your child who is gone, it is something to do, to focus your thoughts. I know the old adage that if you think about something often enough, you will see it everywhere. If you are trying to get pregnant, you'll see pregnant ladies far more often. If you want a blue Mazda, they'll suddenly be everywhere on the road. I don't care – I liked the idea of finding heart shapes and feeling a connection to Tom. Quite frankly, whatever helps.

So, when deciding on a pendant that would hold a part of Thomas, it made sense that I would choose a heart. I'm truly not a big fan of heart-shaped jewellery; it makes me think of what a 12-year-old girl would wear. I ended up choosing a teardrop shaped pendant with an embossed heart at the bottom right corner. This pendant has been so valuable to me this year. I wear it everywhere and have pretty much decided that I need not buy another necklace again. I've been told that I play with it whenever I talk about Thomas and people know when I'm thinking of him because I rub it and will randomly give it a kiss. Whenever I am hit with a trigger, I grab at it and squeeze it in my fist and roll it around between my fingers, while I send up a quick prayer to Tom for help. I now know the benefits of a talisman and I recommend it to anyone struggling with grief or any battle. It might help you find some solid ground.

The phrase 'solid ground' brings me to the final song that I want to share. It is one that is relevant to my current emotional space, and really ever since January. It's almost like I'm coming full circle. The first song I wrote about was also by Ben Abraham and here I am again. Maybe I just love his words and his music. I just don't understand how these songwriters like Ben Abraham and Sara Bareilles can find the words to perfectly depict what I'm going through. **"Satellite"** is such a calm and steady song. It sits at a moderate tempo and dynamic. The piano accompaniment has a muffled tone which resembles my steady plodding along, doing the best I can. The constant rhythm is the time that doesn't stop and I now walk along with this fractured soul that is a new part of me. The strings feel like the build of grief and then they fade or lift to a relieved cadence. The poetry reflects the struggles I fight in my heart but the words are written in a way that is more intimate and subdued in comparison to when the raw wound was inflicted. My world still crashes down but in a manageable way. I can have my 'moments' and then come back into my life, my new normal. I think of my Thomas pendant as my solid ground. A solid ground which is further held up by Owen and Cam and all those that support me. I relate Tom's spirit to this satellite that I call on and look for in the sky when I'm hurting. I imagine, this is Tom singing these words to me, trying to help me through.

When I was a teenager and perhaps even as a younger kid, I used to have nightmares about falling. Falling in the dark. These dreams would wake me with jolting legs and a gasp of horror. On a trip up to Cairns with my sisters and my dad when I was about 18 or so, I decided I wanted to try bungee-jumping. There was a beautiful spot in the hinterland called Kuranda. The tower reached up over the canopy of rainforest and you could see out to the coast. Below was a small natural pool of water, apparently popular for those who wanted to be 'dunked'. My fear of heights and fear of falling was going to end that day, I had decided. I was white with terror as I bunny hopped off the ledge. I was far more relaxed when I jumped the second time, still high on the adrenaline and exhilaration of my first go. From that day onwards I haven't had those falling dreams.

Recently though, I did. It was different. I wasn't falling in the dark. This time I was free-falling as if I'd jumped from a plane. I could vividly see the earth below and the wind rushing up at my face and through my hair. I didn't dream about the moment I jumped; I only came into the dream once I was well into the plummet. I took in my situation and realised I had no parachute. I realised this was my end. At no time did extreme panic hit like it does in nightmares. In front of me was a beautiful green landscape of fields and trees and creeks shining in the sunlight. The wind was fresh in my face and the sky was blue above and around me. I was coming closer and closer to the ground, but I started to smile. I closed my eyes and spread out my arms. I wasn't scared of death. I would see my Thomas again. He would be there to welcome me. That is my hope.

This dream does not mean that I am suicidal. It's ok guys. I'm not rocking in the corner, popping the pills and lost in a depth of depression that would cause alarm. I don't want to die, and I am not seeking it out. I just find that where I used to fear my death, worry about missing out on things I would want to do…I now feel at peace with the possibility. I can't even call death a possibility, it's a guarantee. It's coming one day for all of us. My Thomas has been through it. I can go through it. I have no idea if, when my time on this world is about to end, my feelings will be different in that moment, but for now, I'm ok with it. I don't know if I believe in heaven or reincarnation or the black stuff of nothingness as the next step after death. It doesn't really matter – there is nothing I can do to change it so I will instead find comfort in the utopia that I want to believe: I will be with my Thomas again.

In the closing chapters of the book 'Any Ordinary Day' (Sales, 2018), the author explores the long-term effects on people who have lived through a cataclysmic event. The type of experience which deals with significant trauma. Some people are impacted with a now commonly known consequence, Post-Traumatic Stress Disorder (PTSD). This is experienced fair more frequently in the fields of defence and security, so the armed forces, police, etc. This is due to the extreme nature of these jobs, and even more the fact that trauma is more likely to occur when people are knowingly placed again and again in a position of high danger. Sales has found research to suggest there is another possible outcome for trauma and grief victims that have experienced it as isolated events. It is called 'posttraumatic growth'.

Posttraumatic growth is defined as 'the aspects of positive, personal change a person may experience alongside intense suffering after a major life trauma' (Sales, 2018, p. 206). It is seen as a transformation. It does not happen in place of grief; but rather as a possible side-effect. Sales goes on to suggest some factors at play in the development of posttraumatic growth:

- The event must be catastrophic: "The higher the level of stress caused by the event, the greater the potential for change"
- If someone actively engages in reflection and emotional processing of the event: this could be through counselling, writing, interacting with groups of people dealing with the same stressors
- Emotional intelligence and openness
- If someone's background and past allow them to consider this an anomaly

(p. 211-212)

I know I am still on a long road in experiencing my grief and learning to live my life without my son. I still have moments where I still cannot believe he is gone. I said on the day of his funeral:

A TABLE FOR TWO

These last 13 months, I have been your mum, your carer, your nurse, your pillow and your rehab therapist. I am now adrift and shattered to pieces. I am transformed, I am different. I will never be the same.

I have two choices for transformation –

A. Plan A was for Tom to survive. Plan A was for life to be as it was. Clinging to that plan will transform me. I will only soak and drench and drown myself in the heartbreak of his loss. If I were to settle into this choice for an unending length of time, I know it will negatively impact my son Cameron, my marriage, my relationships, my work, my life. If I choose A, the world stops and so do I. If I am honest, that might have been my preference in the weeks following January 9th. It's the choice to give up. It is to choose only woe. Or…

B. To live my best life as a way to honour Tom. If I choose Plan B, the world keeps turning and so must I. It might be a harder road, but it yields the better results:

- *I will* help build resilience in Cameron by modelling it in myself.

- *I will* enact some possible good to come from the injustice of Tom's death.

- *I will* find ways to practice gratitude, actively find my own silver linings and acknowledge them.

- *I will* keep Tom alive in our little corner of the world. I will move forward with him, not move on without him.

- *I will* learn to get past my guilt and to find a life without regret.

To choose Plan B is to choose joy. To find joy somewhere, somehow despite my loss and so this is my choice. Plan B is my intent and my hope. It is memory, legacy and love. I hope that people in such a situation as mine will find the courage and have the support to choose joy.

Perhaps though, it isn't realistic to believe I can move forward with such a black-and-white stance of intent. There will be days along the path I am yet to walk which will see me revisit Plan A for a time. Those moments are when I will not be able to avoid the heartbreak as it creeps up on me. I already find myself talking to Tom as if he is by my shoulder. I say, "Hey Tom, what a gorgeous day it is," or I thank him for painting me such a stunning sunset over the water, or as I suddenly start to weep out of the blue, I ask him for help. These two elements are at the forefront of my life: joy and woe. They will curl and entwine together. Because my son was here and now he is not. So perhaps a more authentic way to look at the future is to accept that I will find myself with a Plan C.

Plan C

A friend suggested to me that perhaps the best plan sits in the combination of the two. So that I will live with plan A and B side by side; interconnected threads, rather than two paths heading in opposite directions. The perfect example is my 'sad little dress'. When I pull on my dress, resplendent with Superhero joy, alongside all this colour is the sorrow of why the dress exists in the first place. 'A clothing for the soul divine' as William Blake said. My challenge is to learn how to keep them in balance and in relationship to each other. In the years to come as I shape my new normal, perhaps I can move forward with grief while I also find the courage and determination to look to the future and honour Tom. For me, with this choice I make moving forward with my grief – I will still have Tom in my life. In our lives. That is my hope now.

A TABLE FOR TWO

Joy

Joy and woe are woven fine,
A clothing for the soul divine;
Under every grief and pine
Runs a joy with silken twine.
It is right, it should be so;
Man was made for joy and woe;
And when this we rightly know,
Safely through the world we go.

William Blake 'Auguries of Innocence' (1863)

BIG HAND, LITTLE HAND

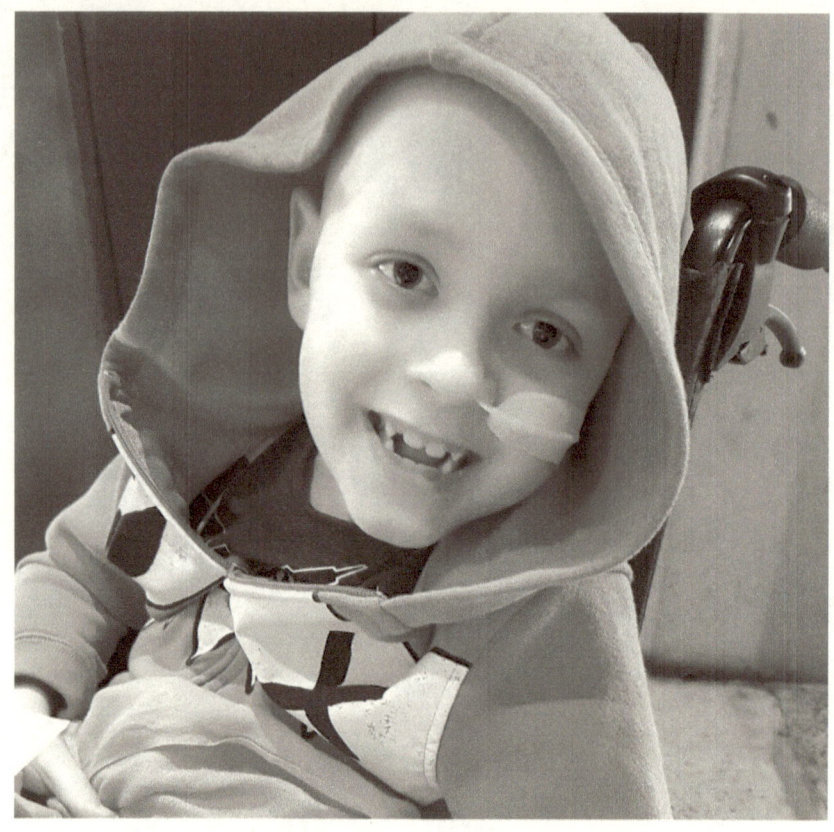

My Hero, My Tom
20th January, 2011 – 9th January, 2019

Practical Advice:

- Be kind to yourself. It will be so hard but your child is your inspiration to get through this.

- Develop photo books and video compilations – one for siblings, one for your child's battle, one for you encompassing all those favourite memories from birth to death.

- If you have the energy, pick a project for commemoration or legacy. It can be small. Fundraise, blog, volunteer, raise awareness, etc.

- A talisman has been really helpful to me – my Tom necklace, my teardrop pendant. Consider what you could keep with you and if it might be a help when a trigger sets you off.

- If you are interested in trauma therapy, find a psychologist that practices EMDR therapy.

- Supporters: observe your friend's child's birthdays and their anniversaries each year. Support any legacy projects your friend might get involved in. When they are ready for it - buy them the book 'Any Ordinary Day' by Leigh Sales, and further down the track - buy them the book 'Gifts from Grief' by Rachel Pope.

Acknowledgments

Writing this book has been quite the rollercoaster. I knew I had one chance to write it and it had to be this year. Most of the time I was squinting though tears and surrounded by piles of decimated tissues. I feel so proud and relieved to have finished this book – it has been an important project for me and I hope it provides others with a story that can help them in tough times.

I have dedicated this book to my son, Thomas. He is my hero and I will love and miss him for all my days. Now, I want to acknowledge his brother Cameron. Thank you Cam for looking after me, giving my neck a rub when it was sore, giving me cuddles when I've been crying over Thomas. This has been a difficult year for all of us but you are my strength. I hope I can help you whenever you find yourself grieving for your brother. Please know that you and Tom spent your youth laughing together, learning together and I hope you can keep those memories strong as you grow up and build a future. Where would I be without your affectionate nature, your reminders of Thomas and your lively spirit? You keep me honest, you keep me smiling and I am so fortunate to have such a wonderful boy.

I need to say how grateful I am for my mum. Thank you, Mum, for supporting me in my journey as a parent, as a carer and in my grief. My care of Tom was inspired by your care of me and I love you dearly. Your face and your words give me comfort and I don't think you realise how important you are to me and the significance of your impact on the person that I have become. I thank my dad also and pray that he is watching out for my boy.

None of this would have been possible without my wonderful husband, Owen. You love me without condition, and you have supported this endeavour every step of the way. You have been my sounding-board, you have been my biggest fan. You were witness to the fight Thomas took on and you have shared in my grief. Thanks for listening, for holding me up, for finding ways to get me laughing. I am honoured to share this life with you.

I'm eternally grateful to my sisters, family and friends who helped me survive the story as it unfolded and encouraged me to get it onto the page. To those friends who continue to find ways to recognise the substance of my grief this year and in the years to come, I am truly grateful. Especially my three girls up close: Danielle, Sharon and Emma who were always at the end of a bottle of wine, the end of the phone line and the end of a box of tissues – through it all, you are my people, you are my hug. I want to acknowledge my employer, Brisbane Catholic Education, my teaching colleagues at Clairvaux MacKillop College, Simon Watson and Ben van Trier - thank you for your support over 2018-2019. I count my blessings to be surrounded by so many friends and supporters, near and far. Too many to name but to all of those cheering me on, I heard you and I am so thankful.

In writing this book, I went on the search for clarification and insight into the medical world, the importance of care and the process of grief. I found answers in my interviews with the wonderful Dr Steve Foresto, Karen Joy, Karen Blue, Tasha Mary and Elham Day. Thank you so much for taking the time to help me get it right and give me a deeper understanding of what we went through. Every day you make an impact on families and you should feel very proud of what you contribute to the world.

ACKNOWLEDGMENTS

A very kind friend assisted me in the research which underpins some of the appendices and the chapters specific to medulloblastoma and posterior fossa syndrome. Dr Narelle Eggins has tirelessly scoured every source of information, data and research there is about these conditions. She agreed with me that a detailed, yet accessible appendix of clinical information was an important addition to this book. As a team we wanted to ensure this book could benefit families who might be new to such a world of childhood brain cancer, treatment and brain injury. We hope they might find some answers and opportunities for clarification within. Narelle, I am very grateful for your contribution to Big Hand, Little Hand and your support of me and my family.

This story encompassed a 13-month battle, most of it in and around the auspices of Lady Cilento Children's Hospital in Brisbane. To the doctors, the nurses, the speechies, the OT's, the physios, the social workers, the teachers, the wardies, the cleaners, the volunteers...to all of you: thank you for your care of Tom, your patience, expertise, creativity and your compassion. I hope you remember Tom and I pray that you continue to help families like ours navigate the unsteadying waters of illness and injury.

To everyone in the Ultimate 48 Hour Author Team: Nat, Stuart and Vivienne. Your logistical advice, your encouragement to keep me to timelines and your attention to detail have helped me achieve my goal. Big Hand, Little Hand was in my hands before Tom's first anniversary and I am proud of this book as an authentic tribute to my son and his legacy. Also, a big thank you to my friends, Trudi, Helen and Jane who helped me with drafting, structural editing and literary feedback – you gave me the confidence to be sure the book was good enough to immortalise my beautiful boy.

Appendix 1

Brain Cancer

Hydrocephalus & Medulloblastoma

Hydrocephalus

Definition
Hydrocephalus is the term used to describe when the ventricles are enlarged due to an increase in pressure of the cerebro-spinal fluid within them.

The ventricles are cavities within the brain that contain cerebrospinal fluid which is continually produced and circulates around the brain and spinal cord, cushioning the brain, providing nutrients, and removing waste products; and then drains back into the blood system of the body. Tumours in the posterior fossa area of the brain can grow into the nearby cerebrospinal fluid drainage pathways, thus blocking the drainage system. The resulting build up of cerebrospinal fluid causes increased intracranial pressure and dilates the ventricles[30,25,] which can damage the brain and eventually become life threatening.

Clinical Symptoms
Classic symptoms of increased ICP include:

- Irritability
- Lethargy
- Some vomiting
- Headaches
- Loss of appetite
- Abnormal eye movements
- Abnormal head posturing (tilted head)
- Behavioral changes
- Seizures

The development of hydrocephalus and the appearance of these symptoms is often what alerts doctors to the possibility of a tumour, and to the diagnosis. However, because these symptoms can be vague, diagnosis can often be delayed.

Statistics[18]: Lam summarises various research findings on the incidence of hydrocephalus in relation to tumours in the posterior fossa area. Because these tumours begin in the area anatomically close to the drainage pathways, hydrocephalus is common 18 occurring in 71–90% of children with posterior fossa tumours. Hydrocephalus after tumour resection occurs in 10–36% of cases, with a worldwide average of 30%.[18,31]

Management
CFS pressure reduction options[18]:

- Place an external ventricular drain (EVD) - temporary
- Insert a ventriculoperitoneal shunt (VPS) - permanent
- Perform an endoscopic third ventriculostomy (ETV) - permanent

A VP shunt is a cerebrospinal fluid diversion device, basically a tube, having a pressure-regulating valve that carries cerebrospinal fluid from the ventricular system to be absorbed by another part of the body outside the brain such as the peritoneum[14] or occasionally, to the pleura of the lungs or the atrium of the heart.

External ventricular drain: EVD: Advantages[18]:

- May avoid exposing patients to unnecessary surgery
- Provides external control over drainage at the time of resection surgery
- Allows removal of resection-related blood and protein products

Disadvantages:
- Increased risk of infection
- Temporary measure (1-2 weeks)

Vertriculoperitioneal Shunt (VPS)

Advantages[18,8]:
- Reduced incidence of post-resection hydrocephalus
- Allows resection surgery to be delayed
- Reduced likelihood of needing external CSF diversion and thus reduced infection risk
- Reducing risk of CSF leak after surgery

Disadvantages:
- May not be permanently needed so the placement surgery was unnecessary

- Does not allow external drainage of blood products after the resection
- VPS have complications such as failure, infection, blockage, etc.
- A VPS has life-long implications for limitations on types of safe activities etc. eg. no contact sport.

Useful website : https://www.healthline.com/health/ventriculoperitoneal-shunt

Medulloblastoma

Medulloblastomas (MB) are aggressive, malignant tumours of the cerebellum that occur mostly in children (peak age of diagnosis is 6 to 8 years), but can develop in teenagers and, more rarely, in adults. They make up about 20% of paediatric brain cancers[27]; and are the most common malignant brain tumour in children. It has been described as the 'poster child' of paediatric brain tumour research with the discovery over the last 15 years that it isn't a single entity, but rather a group of diseases with unique characteristics.

However, medulloblastomas are not all the same in biological make up. Four groups of MB have been described which differ from each other on genetic analysis, age at onset, and prognosis[27]. These groups: WNT, Sonic hedgehog (SHH), Group 3, and Group 4; have been incorporated into the World Health Organisation classification of central nervous system tumours[22]. At this stage, study is being undertaken to increase understanding of the biology of each group so that treatment can be better targeted and thus more effective. In ongoing research, even further heterogeneity or variance is being explored and subtypes within each group, particularly Groups 3, and 4,[24] and the SHH Group[27] have been suggested.

Three-quarters of medulloblastomas arise from the cerebellar vermis and tend to spread along the cerebrospinal fluid pathways, in due course protruding into the fourth ventricle[25].

Diagnosis
Diagnosis is based on[27]:

- Clinical symptoms, often of hydrocephalus
- MRI of the brain and total spine to assess the primary tumour and screen for larger metastases
- Analysis of CSF to screen for tiny metastases
- Histopathological and molecular analysis

Clinical symptoms
These tumours grow relatively rapidly and symptoms evolve over weeks to a few months[25], but often tend to be rather vague and general and so are not easily identified as suggestive of a brain tumour. Children have usually seen a GP 2 or 3 times before presenting at the hospital. These earlier symptoms are those of hydrocephalus caused by the tumour blocking the flow of cerebrospinal fluid as discussed above. In infants, the increase in intracranial pressure (ICP) may lead to a slightly enlarged head as the sutures remain open up until 18 months of age. Thus the usual symptoms of ICP are delayed, resulting in a delayed diagnosis[27]. A combination of the signs and symptoms of increased intracranial pressure plus those of cerebellar dysfunction, can be present[25].

- Unbalanced walking (truncal ataxia)
- Difficulty with rapid alternating movements (appendicular ataxia)
- Double vision (diplopia)

Back pain and incontinence (if tumour has spread to the spine)

Useful website:
https://www.stjude.org/disease/medulloblastoma.html.

Imaging

An MRI of the brain and spinal cord is undertaken and the cerebrospinal fluid analysed to identify the primary tumour, and screen for all metastases. Based on all of these results, the stage of the tumour is assessed on a 5 level scale.

Laboratory Testing

Laboratory testing on a tumour sample after resection is necessary to identify the tumour as medulloblastoma and the group of medulloblastoma it is in[27].

Movements towards improving diagnostic timelines:

Since children diagnosed when the tumour is at a limited stage and localised had statistically significant higher survival rates than those diagnosed at an advanced stage[38], early diagnosis is important. This would help particularly considering consequences such as hydrocephalus (and its associated risk). There are higher survival rates for localised disease rather than metastatic disease.

The Brain Tumour Charity have produced an excellent educational initiative in the UK called Headsmart, targeted at clinicians but also the general public, raising awareness about signs and symptoms that could suggest possible brain tumour. This initiative has made an impressive reduction in the time to diagnosis for patients with brain tumours. Due to its success similar educational programs are being developed internationally.

Headsmart: https://www.headsmart.org.uk/

Treatment
Treatment may vary with the age and presentation of the child in terms of the stage of development of the cancer; the extent of the surgical resection, the biology of the tumour eg., MYC amplification, and which of the four groups their medulloblastoma falls into.

Surgery
If hydrocephalus is evident on MRI, the initial procedure may be surgery to relieve the intracranial pressure as discussed above. In almost all cases, the tumour will be resected surgically usually with the aim of removing as much as possible of the tumour mass.

If hydrocephalus is present after surgery, further action may need to be taken to reduce the ICP. Typically this would mean implanting a VP Shunt.

Rehabilitation might be required post-surgery and is targeted to suit each child's areas of need, may involve physiotherapy, occupational and speech therapy, and can be ongoing during the medical treatment to work on restoring functioning. Particularly if the child has acquired brain injury as a result of the surgery (see Appendix 2 for more information).

Radiation and Chemotherapy
When the child has recovered from the surgery, radiation therapy will usually be administered. Tom was given 30 sessions of craniospinal irradiation with a boost to the tumour bed. This is followed by chemotherapy, with doses of each depending on which main group and subtype the medulloblastoma falls into.

Standard – the chemotherapy protocol prescribed for Tom was standard. Cyclophosphamide, Vincristine, Cisplatin, doxorubicin. Amifostine was an associated medication which acted as a cytoprotectant. This drug would try to help normal body tissues protect the kidneys from damaging effects of cisplatin. The cycle allowed for recovery time at the end of a 28-day cycle.

Variance on this standard protocol would be dependent on the level of risk the tumour presented, the age of the patient, surgical outcomes and whether the tumour was metastatic at presentation.

Side Effects

The side effects listed are possibilities but not every child will get every side effect. Some may present and others may not. There may be different side effects seen depending on which cycle the child is on. Those listed as 'common' are likely to affect 80% of children, 'occasional' are likely to affect 20% of children and 'rare' are likely to affect 5% of children. Side effects with an Asterix (*) – toxicity may occur after completion of therapy

Cyclophosphomide (CPM):
Immediate - Within 1-2 days

Common   Loss of appetite, nausea and vomiting

Occasional Metallic taste*, stomach discomfort and diarrhoea

Rare   Temporary blurred vision, stuffy nose, rash, abnormal heart rhythm, severe allergic reaction, SIADH: abnormal hormone function, affecting salt levels and urine output

Prompt - Within 2-3 weeks (prior to next cycle)

Common   Lower than normal white blood cells count, hair loss and reduced function of the immune system

Occasional Low red blood cell and platelet count and bleeding from the bladder*

Rare   Heart damage, bleeding into and inflammation of the heart muscle, changes in skin colour, nail changes and impaired wound healing

Delayed – anytime later during therapy
Common   Absence of sperm or fewer sperm than normal (prolonged or permanent), infertility*

Occasional Absence or cessation of menstruation

Rare   Cessation of of normal functioning of the ovaries (infertility)* and damage/scarring and inflammation of lung tissue*

Late: After completion of treatment
Rare   A new leukemia or cancer and scarring of the bladder

Vincristine (VCR):
Immediate - Within 1-2 days
Occasional Jaw pain and headaches

Rare   Damage to nearby tissue if the medication leaks from the vein

Prompt - Within 2-3 weeks (prior to next cycle)

Common   Constipation and temporary hair loss

Occasional Abdominal pain or cramps, muscle weakness, decrease in the number of red and white blood cells and platelets made in the bone marrow

Rare   Slowing of intestinal activity resulting in vomiting and/or constipation, SIADH, drooping eyelids, double vision, night blindness, hoarseness, difficulty breathing and seizures

Delayed – anytime later during therapy

Common   Loss of reflexes in the arms and legs

Occasional Numbness, tingling or pain in the hands and feet, clumsiness, wrist or foot drop, abnormal walking action

Rare Difficulty walking, dizziness, vertigo, hearing loss, blindness and painful or difficult urination

Cisplatin:
Immediate - Within 1-2 days
Common Nausea* and vomiting*

Occasional Metallic taste*

Rare Severe allergic reaction (swelling in the face, wheezing, rapid heart rate and abnormally low blood pressure), inflammation of a vein, damage to nearby tissue if the medication leaks from the vein

Prompt - Within 2-3 weeks (prior to next cycle)

Common Loss of appetite*, decrease in the number of red and white blood cells and platelets made in the bone marrow, abnormally low magnesium level in the blood*, kidney damage* and high frequency hearing loss*

Occasional Abnormal levels of some salts in the blood (sodium, potassium)*, abnormal nerve function in the feet/ankles and hand/wrists – includes numbness, weakness, burning pain (especially at night) and loss of reflexes*

Rare Damage to the middle ear that can cause balance problems and dizziness, ringing in the ears*, rash, seizures and increased liver enzymes in the blood*

BRAIN CANCER

<u>Delayed – anytime later during therapy</u>

Occasional   Hearing loss in the normal range

Rare   Absence of reflexes, inability to recognise stimuli from the brain and sense of the relative position of neighbouring parts of the body*, inflammation or swelling of the optic nerve, blurred vision, blindness, altered colour vision, deafness and kidney failure

These drugs are not chemotherapy drugs but are given in association
Amifostine: a cytoprotectant
<u>Immediate – Within 1-2 days</u>

Common   Nausea, vomiting, flushing, abnormally low blood pressure

Occasional   Sleepiness, dizziness and sneezing

Rare   Hiccups and chills

<u>Prompt – Within 2-3 weeks (prior to next cycle)</u>

Occasional   Low level of calcium (when given for several days or several times per day)

Rare   Rash

Mesna:
<u>Immediate – Within 1-2 days</u>

Common   Bad taste when taken by mouth

Occasional   Nausea, vomiting, stomach pain, fatigue, headaches

Rare   Facial flushing/redness, rash, fever, pain in arms/legs and joints, temporary low blood pressure, rapid heart rate, dizziness, anxiety, confusion, swelling around the eyes, cough and sever allergic reaction

<u>Prompt – Within 2-3 weeks</u>
Occasional Diarrhoea

Side Effects source: Taken from the literature provided to families by Queensland Paediatric Haematology Oncology Network (QPHON)

A general side effect from chemotherapy is **Neutropenia**:

Neutropenia is the medical term for a decrease in the number of a particular type of circulating white blood cells called neutrophils. Neutrophils are a very important part of the immune system and play an important role in protecting the body against bacterial infections. Chemotherapy-induced neutropenia (CIN) is the most serious hematological toxicity of cancer chemotherapy.[3]

http://melbournehaematology.com.au/fact-sheets/neutropenia.html

Outcomes

The outcome and prognosis for a patient with medulloblastoma is related to many factors:

- The size of the tumour, which effects the extent of surgical resection,
- the part of the brain impacted by the tumour and the surgery
- the absence/presence of metastases at the time of diagnosis
- the age of the child
- the absence/presence of posterior fossa syndrome and/or cerebullar mutism syndrome - see Appendix 2 for further detail

- the group and subtype the tumour falls into which determines the amount of radiation and the type of chemotherapy the child receives

At this point, The WNT group of medulloblastomas have a much better prognosis because the tumours are responsive to treatment, while the other groups have a blood brain barrier which makes them more resistant to treatment.

Quality of Life

Though the overall *mean* survival rates for medulloblastoma are steadily increasing, being currently around 70-80% for standard risk and 60% for high risk patients, there is an increasing focus on the quality of life for these children and the issues they face because of brain damage resulting from both the medulloblastoma and the treatment[5,35,13]. Impacts can include:

- The development of chemotherapy-induced toxicity in the central nervous system
- Possible deficits in aspects of cognitive function, which can include attention difficulties, working memory, low processing speed, intellect, academic achievement, and emotional health[13,5].

However there appear to be differences between how parents and health care professionals evaluate survival outcomes. In the tradeoff between survival and degree of disability, parents tend to choose survival; but in contrast, providers were concerned about levels of disability[16].

Parents also tended to emphasise the importance of social functioning over academic ability[11]. Some studies found the quality of life reported by survivors of childhood medulloblastoma and their carers was in the normal range despite the degree of disability[23].

There is a range of possible quality of life issues for survivors of MB, but the outcome is individual for each child of course according to many of the factors mentioned above.

For a detailed review on the reported quality of life after surviving medulloblastoma see[5] https://www.ncbi.nlm.nih.gov/pmc/articles/PMC6655396

Investigations into the long-term consequences of brain tumours in the posterior fossa region, and of the treatment-related side effects are ongoing.

Current Research
St Jude's Trial: SJMB12

An international trial based out of the USA which focuses their research on tailoring treatment using historical data and tumour histology/pathology. They aim to categorize patient cases into different pathways – and therefore different protocols. The research is built on historical data and countries around the world contribute data to this trial.

https://www.stjude.org/disease/medulloblastoma.html.

The great hope with this ever expanding knowledge is to be able to develop personalised therapies which will cure more children and have less toxicity.

Statistics for medulloblastoma (these tend to vary between different studies and are here as an indication only)

- An approximate occurrence of 5 cases per 1 million individuals per year. This equates to roughly 10 children a month being diagnosed in Australia alone and accounts for 20% of pediatric brain tumours[27].

- Peak age of diagnosis is 6-8 years but can occur at any age[27].
- 5 year survival rate for standard risk patients is 70%-85% (standard risk: older than age 3, gross total tumour resection, non-metastatic at diagnosis).
- Rare in adults. 0.05 cases per 100,000 individuals.
- 5 year survival rate for metastatic medulloblastoma and residual tumour not removed greater than 1.5cm^2 is approximately 60%.
- Gender ratio 1.8: 1 male : female, but varies within the 4 groups.
- Approximately 18% of patients develop other cancers within 30 years of medulloblastoma diagnosis.
- No ethnic or geographic differences found.

Where to find ongoing information:

- Cancer Council QLD: https://cancerqld.org.au/research/queensland-cancer-statistics/accr/
- The Australian Paediatric Cancer Registry: www.cancerqld.org.au/research/cancer-registries/australian-childhood-cancer-registry
- Centre for Brain Tumour Research in the USA, UK, https://www.braintumourresearch.org

Further Research

A better understanding of genetic composition of the varying MB groups and their subtypes will enable the development of better targeted and more effective treatments[24,19,28] and, as mentioned above, many researchers are focussing on this issue. Researchers are also looking into a more integrated view of the brain that accounts for the interactive structural and functional role of the cerebellum, the cortex and their connectivity[37]. Investigations into the long-term consequences of brain tumours in the posterior fossa region, and of the treatment-related side effects are ongoing.

Work is also being undertaken on understanding how the disease spreads and recurs by examining possible molecular pathways[15], and genetic divergence between primary tumours and their metastases. While spread has been thought to be via the CSF[7], suggested dissemination could be via the blood.

Appendix 2
Brain Injury
Posterior Fossa Syndrome &
Cerebellar Mutism Syndrome

Posterior Fossa Syndrome

Medulloblastomas develop in the posterior fossa region of the brain and, as discussed above, treatment involves surgical resection of the tumour. Neurosurgeons may strive to remove the entire tumour whenever possible as research had suggested the extent of the removal is an indicator of the outcome of the disease for the patient. However, a consequence of surgery in this brain region can be posterior fossa syndrome (PFS), sometimes referred to as cerebellar mutism syndrome which occurs in up to 29% of medulloblastoma patients following surgery[32].

Definition
(Posterior fossa syndrome-cerebellar mutism appears to be defined by its symptoms only, at present, because the exact cause is not fully understood).

The following is taken from the official definition of the syndrome developed from an international, interdisciplinary conference conducted by the Iceland Delphi Group, and published in 2016. (Medical terminology is explained below)

Post-operative paediatric *posterior fossa syndrome-cerebellar mutism* is characterised by:

- Mutism/reduced speech. Speech production that is reduced and limited to single words or short sentences that can only be elicited after vigorous stimulation (dysprosodia)
- Impairment of gait (ataxia)
- Extreme coordination (dysmetria)
- Impaired or inability to swallow (oropharyngeal dysfunction/dysphagia)
- Tremor
- Low muscle strength (hypotonia)
- Emotional lability (constantly changing emotions) after cerebellar or 4th ventricle tumour surgery in children. In practice, these children can be inconsolable, apathetic, and/or hypokinetic[34] for a period of time
- Impairments in executive function
- Impairments in visual-spatial abilities
- Urinary retention/incontinence and hemiparesis

It may frequently be accompanied by cerebellar motor syndrome[b], cerebellar cognitive affective syndrome[c] and brain stem dysfunction including long tract signs[d] and cranial neuropathies. The mutism is always transient, but recovery may be prolonged. Speech and language may not return to normal, and other deficits of cognitive, affective and motor function often persist [9]."

Risk Factors[2]

Several studies have identified possible risk factors, but the evidence is inconsistent. Avula et al concluded that PSF-CMS was likely to result from several rather than a single factor, with "direct injury from surgery being a major one". Direct surgical damage to *posterior fossa syndrome* - related anatomical substrates is regarded as the most likely cause for PFS by a number of authors[2].

Possible Pre-Operative factors (summarised in Avula, S., et al)[2]

- Medulloblastomas patients are at higher risk than patients with other brain tumours
- Midline location of the tumour[17]
- Evidence of brainstem invasion and/or compression
- Age of child
- Diameter of tumour greater than or equal 5 cm[29]
- Involvement of the Vermis (The vermis is the unpaired, median part of the cerebellum that connects the two hemispheres of the brain)

Because the syndrome follows surgery, issues related to the degree of resection, and surgical technique generally have been investigated.

Possible Post-Operative factors related to surgical technique (summarized in Avula, S., et al)[2]

- Aggressive surgical approach[17] with emphasis on resection of the whole tumour
- Injury caused by retractors and the use of instruments such as ultrasonic aspirators.
- Pols et al, (2017)[29] found that a 0.5C increase in average temperature for the first 4 days after surgery (no infection) indicated the patient was 5 times more likely to develop PFS-CM.

Recent data presented by Siu et al. (2013)[2] shows significant reduction in the incidence of posterior fossa syndrome-cerebellar mutism syndrome (39 to 13.5%) with the implementation of the telovelar approach (vermis-sparing surgery), avoidance of the Cavitron Ultrasonic Aspirator (CUSA) and minimising retraction. There is also anecdotal evidence of reduction in PFS-CMS with routine use of electrophysiological monitoring (Wells EM, Khademian ZP, Walsh KS, Vezina G, Sposto R, Keating RF, Packer RJ, 2010)[2].

Treatment
Initially sedation if the child is very distressed.

Ongoing rehabilitation working on speech (including eating) and language, intellectual functioning, and gross and fine motor skills.

Outcomes
Importantly, it becomes obvious from reading the literature that diagnosing PFS-CMS is not a black and white issue, as patients can have this unfortunate outcome of surgery to varying degrees from mild to devastating. This should be kept in mind when considering studies comparing longer term outcomes for patients who had PSF-CMS and those who did not. The types of comparisons following need to be considered in terms of the degree to which individual patients display the syndrome.

Further research
A focus in the research at present is in understanding why *posterior fossa syndrome-cerebellar mutism* occurs and developing a tool for predicting the likelihood of *posterior fossa syndrome-cerebellar mutism* development before surgery.

Advancing imaging technology is being employed successfully. Spiteri et al (2019)[33] have used MR images in 3-D space to identify

7 potential biomarkers for *posterior fossa syndrome-cerebellar mutism* in an automative system.

Lui et al, (2018)[21] have developed a pre-operative scoring system for predicting risk of post-operative paediatric cerebellar mutism syndrome to be used as an indicator for the surgeons and for consideration in consent discussions. This is still in development.

Appendix 3
Palliative Care
Hummingbird House

Hummingbird House is a free service for families who need paediatric hospice care. They are funded through a combination of support from both State and Federal governments, philanthropy, community fundraising and sources such as Medicare.

About Hummingbird House

Hummingbird House (HH) is Queensland's only children's hospice, providing short break stays, family support services, creative therapies, care at the end of life and after-death care (including grief and bereavement support). It is a home-like environment, where kids can be kids, families can reconnect and precious memories can be created. Current statistics estimate around 3,700 Queensland children are living with life-limiting conditions. Diagnosis with a life-limiting condition means a child is not expected to reach their 18th birthday, and in most cases their life expectancy is much shorter. Hummingbird House delivers best-practice paediatric palliative care.

Hummingbird House is an 8-bed facility with 5 family accommodation suites, therapy rooms, multi-sensory room, all-abilities accessible bath, pool, large outdoor spaces and play centre, teenagers retreat, and a specifically designed space for care after death. It is fully accredited under National Healthcare Quality Standards September 2012, and AS/NZS ISO 9001 2016, making us the only private licensed paediatric palliative care facility in Australia. The HH team includes: nurses, personal care workers, doctors, family support workers, housekeepers, cooks, art therapist, and allied health staff.

Since opening in late 2016, they have supported over 221 families. This has included providing overnight respite care for more than 3200 bed days, including: stepdown stays where the child has been admitted directly from hospital; symptom management stays (thereby avoiding a hospital admission); care at the end of life for 31 children; and specialised after-death care (including family bereavement support and funeral planning) for 26 children whose families chose to come to HH after their child's death. Our major referrer is the Paediatric Palliative Care Service at the Queensland Children's Hospital.

The Impact of Hummingbird House – A Children's Hospice

Hummingbird House offers families choice: care in their home or in the hospice, by working with the child's entire family and broader social circle, providing support for the child's care and the family's grief and bereavement. With the operational costs for the hospice assured, Hummingbird House will continue to provide care for families in the south-east corner of Queensland.

PALLIATIVE CARE

This will allow them to refine and expand the state-wide reach of the service through the delivery of care in the child's community. In all aspects of the service Hummingbird House provides, they connect children with the right care at the right time in the right place. Thereby giving families the option of greater choice over what is important to them and their child.

Hummingbird House has changed how children with life-limiting conditions live and die. This has only been achieved through our strong and successful partnership with both State and Federal Governments as well as dedicated fundraising efforts by our staff, as well as by community organisations, community members and families.

www.hummingbirdhouse.org.au

Appendix 4

Other Support Services and Charities

(Australia)

This is a list of websites and organisations dedicated to supporting families dealing with childhood cancer and grief. Your social worker, the oncology team and the palliative care department at your hospital will also be able to provide resources, literature and other support options.

Australian and New Zealand Children's Haematology/Oncology Group

ANZCHOG's primary purpose is to improve outcomes for children and adolescents with cancer and associated blood diseases through quality research, facilitation of innovative paediatric clinical trials and promotion of best practice in clinical care.

www.anzchog.org

Australian Centre for Grief and Bereavement
ACGB is funded by the Department of Health to provide a statewide, specialist bereavement service for individuals, children and families who need assistance following the death of someone close to them.

www.grief.org.au

Brain Child Foundation
To provide support and better tomorrows to the children and families affected by brain and spinal cord tumours while striving for a cure.

www.brainchild.org.au

Camp Quality
Camp Quality gives kids facing cancer the chance to be kids again. Our services and programs are made specifically to help kids aged 0-13 who are dealing with their own diagnosis, or the diagnosis of someone they love, like a brother, sister, mum or dad.

www.campquality.org.au

Cancer Australia – Children's cancer website
This is a website dedicated to all sufferers of cancer. There is a specific link on this website to children's cancer. You will find information, practical advice, clinical trials and research as well as where to go for emotional support.

www.canceraustralia.gov.au

OTHER SUPPORT SERVICES AND CHARITIES

Cancer Council Queensland
A website focusing on cancer in general with information about every different type of cancer. You can find the most recent data relating to research and statistics on this site as well as information around prevention, support and treatment.

www.cancerqld.org.au

CanTeen
This organisation is dedicated to young people (12-25) who are experiencing or are impacted by cancer.

www.canteen.org.au

Childhood Cancer Support (accommodation)
Childhood Cancer Support is a not-for-profit organisation who is dedicated to providing families affected by childhood cancer with a place to live that looks and feels like home. This organisation provides a safe and family-focused environment for regional families whilst their child receives life-saving cancer treatment in Brisbane at the Queensland Children's Hospital.

www.ccs.org.au

Children's Oncology Group
The Children's Oncology Group (COG), a National Cancer Institute supported clinical trials group, is the world's largest organization devoted exclusively to childhood and adolescent cancer research. The COG unites more than 9,000 experts in childhood cancer at more than 200 leading children's hospitals, universities, and cancer centers across North America, Australia, New Zealand, and Europe in the fight against childhood cancer.

www.childrensoncologygroup.org

Compassionate Friends
The Compassionate Friends is an international self-help support organisation for bereaved parents, siblings and grandparents grieving for the loss of a child.

www.compassionatefriendsqld.org.au

CureSearch
CureSearch for Children's Cancer is a U.S.-based non-profit foundation that accelerates the search for cures for children's cancer by driving innovation, overcoming research barriers and solving the field's most challenging problems.

www.curesearch.org

Grief Link
Grief Link provides information for people who are dealing with the grief caused by the death of someone close to them, and for those who are supporting them. Provides important resources and reading material.

www.grieflink.org.au

Kids With Cancer
A fundraising organisation which provides assistance to doctors, nurses, families, researchers and support groups involved in caring for the youngest of children suffering with all childhood cancers. The money we raise and the donations we receive are allocated to benefit: public hospitals (with children's oncology units) research units and families who find themselves placed in financial difficulties, due to their child being treated for cancer.

www.kidswithcancer.org.au

OTHER SUPPORT SERVICES AND CHARITIES

Leukaemia Foundation
The Leukaemia Foundation is the only national charity dedicated to helping those with leukaemia, lymphoma, myeloma and related blood disorders survive and then live a better quality of life.

www.leukaemia.org.au

Lifeline
Lifeline is a national charity providing all Australians experiencing a personal crisis with access to 24 hour crisis support and suicide prevention services.

www.lifeline.org.au

Make a Wish
Wishes are an essential complement to a child's medical treatment - with the power to positively impact the lives of sick kids, their families and communities.

www.makeawish.org.au

Redkite
A charitable organisation which provides essential support to children, teenagers and young adults with cancer to ensure the best possible quality of life for them and their family – now and into the future.

www.redkite.org.au

Ronald McDonald House Charities

When a child is diagnosed with a serious illness, it impacts the whole family. Lives can be turned upside down. Ronald McDonald House provide a range of programs to help families stay together and close to the care they need, including accommodation for regionally based families, retreats and education support.

www.rmhc.org.au

Starlight Foundation

The Starlight programs are an essential part of a child's total care. Their work complements traditional medical treatment by helping young people flourish, build resilience and shape their individuality. Working within hospitals in dedicated facilities and at bedside, Starlight also work in wish-granting and outpatient engagement.

www.starlight.org.au

Reference List

Music: Playlist and song reference information

Chapter 1 - Abraham, Ben. (2016) Home. On *Sirens*, Released by Secretly Canadian.

Chapter 2 - Abraham, Ben. (2016) I Belong To You. On *Sirens*, Released by Secretly Canadian.

Chapter 3 - Imagine Dragons. (2017) Thunder. On *Evolve*, Released by Interscope Records and Kidinakorner. 2017

Chapter 4 - Bareilles, Sara. (2019) Orpheus. On *Amidst the Chaos*, Released by Sony

Chapter 5 - Sinclair J. and Jeberg, J, and co-written by Urie, B, Owen Youngs, J, Pritchard, L, Hollander, S, Lobban-Bean, W, Parks, T and Juber, I. (2018) High Hopes. On *Pray for the Wicked*, Released by Fueled By Ramen and DCD Records.

Chapter 5 - Timberlake, J, Martin, M, Shellback, Kotecha, S, Holter, O. (2016) Hair Up. On *Trolls Soundtrack*. Released by RCA Records.

Note: The theme which provides the backing for this piece is by Edvard Grieg.

Chapter 6 - Higgins, Missy. (2018) Run So Fast. On *The Special Ones*, Released by Eleven: A Music Company.

Chapter 7 - Pasek, B and Paul, J. (2017) This Is Me. On *The Greatest Showman Soundtrack*, Released by Atlantic Records.

Chapter 8 - Steinberg, B and Kelly, T. (1986) True Colours. Re-released on *Trolls Soundtrack* by RCA Records.

Chapter 9 - Jay, Armon. (2015) Shine a Light. On *Del Rio*, Self-release.

Chapter 10 - Bareilles, Sara (2010) Send Me The Moon. On *Kaleidoscope* EP. Released by Amoeba Music.

Chapter 11 - Bareilles, Sara. (2019) No Such Thing. On *Amidst the Chaos*, Released by Sony.

Chapter 12 - Abraham, Ben and Bareilles, Sara. (2019) Satellite. Single release by Atlantic Records (at time of publication).

Other referenced sources:

Langton-Gilks, Sacha, (2018), *Follow The Child*, Jessica Kingsley Publishers, London and Philadelphia.

Pope, Rachel, (2019), *Gifts From Grief*, Chapter 1 Publishers, Australia.

Sales, Leigh, (2018), *Any Ordinary Day*, Penguin, Australia.

REFERENCE LIST

Side Effects source details: for chemotherapy and cytoprotectant drugs as listed in Appendix 1:

Children's Health Queensland Hospital and Health Service, Taken from the literature provided to families by Queensland Paediatric Haematology Oncology Network (QPHON), Adapted from the COG Commercial Agents Monograph v7 (Version Date 4/11/2014). LCCH Review Date January 2016

Research Bibliography for Appendix 1 and 2:

Note: References marked * have open access and can be viewed by the general public

1. *Agarwal, N., Shukla, R., Agarwal, D., Gupta, K., Luthra, R., Gupta, J., & Jain, S. (2017). Pediatric ventriculoperitoneal shunts and their complications: An analysis. *Journal of Indian Association of Pediatric Surgeons, 22*(3), 155-157. doi: 10.4103/0971-9261.207624 http://www.jiaps.com/article.asp?issn=0971- 9261;year=2017;volume=22;issue=3;spage=155;epage=157;aulast=Agarwal

2. *Avula, S., Mallucci, C., Kumar, R., & Pizer, B. (2015). Posterior fossa syndrome following brain tumour resection: review of pathophysiology and a new hypothesis on its pathogenesis. *Child's Nervous System, 31*(10), 1859-1867. doi: 10.1007/s00381-015-2797-0 file:///C:/Users/i5/Documents/My%20EndNote%20Library.Data/1116494336%20tumour%20resection.pdf

3. *Badr, M., Hassan, T., Sakr, H., Karam, N., Rahman, D. A., Shahbah, D., . . . Fehr, S. (2016). Chemotherapy-induced neutropenia among pediatric cancer patients in Egypt: Risks and consequences. *Molecular and clinical oncology, 5*(3), 300-306. doi: 10.3892/mco.2016.957 https://www.ncbi.nlm.nih.gov/pmc/articles/PMC4998081/

4. *Cavalli, F. M. G., Remke, M., Rampasek, L., Peacock, J., Shih, D. J. H., Luu, B., . . . Taylor, M. D. (2017). Intertumoral Heterogeneity within Medulloblastoma Subgroups. *Cancer Cell, 31*(6), 737-754.e736. doi: https://www.ncbi.nlm.nih.gov/pmc/articles/PMC6163053/

5. *Chevignard, M., Câmara-Costa, H., Doz, F., & Dellatolas, G. (2017). Core deficits and quality of survival after childhood medulloblastoma: a review. *Neuro-Oncology Practice, 4*(2), 82-97. doi: 10.1093/nop/npw013 https://www.ncbi.nlm.nih.gov/pmc/articles/PMC6655396/

6. *Dewan, M. C., Lim, J., Shannon, C. N., & Wellons, J. C. (2017). The durability of endoscopic third ventriculostomy and ventriculoperitoneal shunts in children with hydrocephalus following posterior fossa tumor resection: a systematic review and time-to-failure analysis. 19(5), 578. doi: 10.3171/2017.1.peds16536 https://thejns.org/pediatrics/view/journals/j-neurosurg-pediatr/19/5/article-p578.xml

7. *Garzia, L., Kijima, N., Morrissy, A. S., De Antonellis, P., Guerreiro-Stucklin, A., Holgado, B. L., . . . Taylor, M. D. (2018). A Hematogenous Route for Medulloblastoma Leptomeningeal Metastases. *Cell, 172*(5), 1050-1062.e1014. doi: 10.1016/j.cell.2018.01.038 https://www.ncbi.nlm.nih.gov/pmc/articles/PMC6346737/

8. Garcia-Gonzalez, O., & Hernandez-Ponce, P. (2016). NS-31: Endoscopic third ventriculocisternostomy for the treatment of hydrocephalus in children with posterior fossa tumors. *Neuro-Oncology, 18*(Suppl 3), iii133-iii134. doi: 10.1093/neuonc/now078.31 https://www.ncbi.nlm.nih.gov/pmc/articles/PMC4903706/

9. Gudrunardottir, T., Morgan, A. T., Lux, A. L., Walker, D. A., Walsh, K. S., Wells, E. M., . . . Group, F. t. I. D. (2016). Consensus paper on post-operative pediatric cerebellar mutism syndrome: the Iceland Delphi results. [journal article]. *Child's Nervous System, 32*(7), 1195-1203. doi: 10.1007/s00381-016-3093-3

REFERENCE LIST

10. *Hanak, B. W., Bonow, R. H., Harris, C. A., & Browd, S. R. (2017). Cerebrospinal Fluid Shunting Complications in Children. *Pediatric neurosurgery, 52*(6), 381-400. doi: 10.1159/000452840 https://www.ncbi.nlm.nih.gov/pmc/articles/PMC5915307/

11. Henrich, N., Marra, C. A., Gastonguay, L., Mabbott, D., Malkin, D., Fryer, C., . . . Lynd, L. (2014). De-escalation of therapy for pediatric medulloblastoma: Trade-offs between quality of life and survival. *Pediatric Blood & Cancer, 61*(7), 1300-1304. doi: 10.1002/pbc.24990 https://onlinelibrary.wiley.com/doi/abs/10.1002/pbc.24990

12. *Hubbard, A. K., Marcotte, E. L., Fortuna, G., Spector, L. G., & Poynter, J. N. (2019). Trends in International Incidence of Pediatric Cancers in Children Under 5 Years of Age: 1988–2012. *JNCI Cancer Spectrum, 3*(1). doi: 10.1093/jncics/pkz007

13. *Ikonomidou, C. (2018). Chemotherapy and the pediatric brain. *Molecular and cellular pediatrics, 5*(1), 8-8. doi: 10.1186/s40348-018-0087-0 https://www.ncbi.nlm.nih.gov/pmc/articles/PMC6219996/

14. *Junaid, M., Ahmed, M., & Rashid, M. U. (2018). An experience with ventriculoperitoneal shunting at keen's point for hydrocephalus. *Pakistan journal of medical sciences, 34*(3), 691-695. doi: 10.12669/pjms.343.14081 https://www.ncbi.nlm.nih.gov/pmc/articles/PMC6041550/

15. *Kahn, S. A., Wang, X., Nitta, R. T., Gholamin, S., Theruvath, J., Hutter, G., . . . Cheshier, S. H. (2018). Notch1 regulates the initiation of metastasis and self-renewal of Group 3 medulloblastoma. *Nature communications, 9*(1), 4121-4121. doi: 10.1038/s41467-018-06564-9 https://www.ncbi.nlm.nih.gov/pmc/articles/PMC6175869/

16. *Khakban, A., Mohammadi, T., Lynd, L. D., Mabbott, D. J., Bouffet, E., Gastonguay, L., . . . Marra, C. A. (2018). How do

parents and providers trade-off between disability and survival? Preferences in the treatment of pediatric medulloblastoma. *Patient preference and adherence, 12,* 2103-2110. doi: 10.2147/ppa. s168739 https://www.ncbi.nlm.nih.gov/pmc/articles/PMC6188209/

17. *Korah, M. P., Esiashvili, N., Mazewski, C. M., Hudgins, R. J., Tighiouart, M., Janss, A. J., . . . Marcus, R. B., Jr. (2010). Incidence, Risks, and Sequelae of Posterior Fossa Syndrome in Pediatric Medulloblastoma. *International Journal of Radiation Oncology • Biology • Physics, 77*(1), 106-112. doi: 10.1016/j.ijrobp.2009.04.058 https://doi.org/10.1016/j.ijrobp.2009.04.058

18. *Lam, S., Reddy, G. D., Lin, Y., & Jea, A. (2015). Management of hydrocephalus in children with posterior fossa tumors. *Surgical neurology international, 6*(Suppl 11), S346-S348. doi: 10.4103/2152-7806.161413 https://www.ncbi.nlm.nih.gov/pmc/articles/PMC4521311/

19. *Łastowska, M., Trubicka, J., Karkucińska-Więckowska, A., Kaleta, M., Tarasińska, M., Perek-Polnik, M., . . . Matyja, E. (2019). Immunohistochemical detection of ALK protein identifies APC mutated medulloblastoma and differentiates the WNT-activated medulloblastoma from other types of posterior fossa childhood tumors. *Brain tumor pathology, 36*(1), 1-6. doi: 10.1007/s10014-018-0331-2 https://www.ncbi.nlm.nih.gov/pmc/articles/PMC6514113/

20. Li, C., Gui, S., & Zhang, Y. (2017). Compare the safety and efficacy of endoscopic third ventriculostomy and ventriculoperitoneal shunt placement in infants and children with hydrocephalus: a systematic review and meta-analysis. *International Journal of Neuroscience,* 1-30. doi: 10.1080/00207454.2017.1348352 https://doi.org/10.1080/00207454.2017.1348352

21. Liu, J.-F., Dineen, R. A., Avula, S., Chambers, T., Dutta, M., Jaspan, T., . . . Walker, D. A. (2018). Development of a pre-operative scoring system for predicting risk of post-operative paediatric

cerebellar mutism syndrome. *British Journal of Neurosurgery, 32*(1), 18-27. doi: 10.1080/02688697.2018.1431204 https://doi.org/10.1 080/02688697.2018.1431204

22. *Louis, D. N., Perry, A., Reifenberger, G., von Deimling, A., Figarella-Branger, D., Cavenee, W. K., . . . Ellison, D. W. (2016). The 2016 World Health Organization Classification of Tumors of the Central Nervous System: a summary. [journal article]. *Acta Neuropathologica, 131*(6), 803-820. doi: 10.1007/s00401-016-1545-1 https://doi.org/10.100   7/s00401-016-1545-1

23. Maddrey, A. M., Bergeron, J. A., Lombardo, E. R., McDonald, N. K., Mulne, A. F., Barenberg, P. D., & Bowers, D. C. (2005). Neuropsychological performance and quality of life of 10 year survivors of childhood medulloblastoma. [journal article]. *Journal of neuro-oncology, 72*(3), 245-253. doi: 10.1007/s11060-004-3009-z https://doi.org/10.1007/s11060-004-3009-z

24. *Menyhárt, O., Giangaspero, F., & Győrffy, B. (2019). Molecular markers and potential therapeutic targets in non-WNT/non-SHH (group 3 and group 4) medulloblastomas. *Journal of hematology & oncology, 12*(1), 29-29. doi: 10.1186/s13045-019-0712-y https://www.ncbi.nlm.nih.gov/pmc/articles/PMC6420757/

25. *Millard, N. E., & De Braganca, K. C. (2016). Medulloblastoma. *Journal of child neurology, 31*(12), 1341-1353. doi: 10.1177/0883073815600866 https://www.ncbi.nlm.nih.gov/pmc/articles/PMC4995146/

26. *Mohannad Essam Elgamal, Essam A. Elgamal, Anwar Ahmad, Adham Aly Elsayed, Basel Younes, Aljaraki, M. K., & Elholiby, T. I. (2018). atrogenic (Traumatic) Occipital Artery Pseudoaneurysm – Rare Complication of Ventriculoperitoneal Shunt in an Infant: Case Report and Review of the Literature. *Asian J Neurosurg, 13*(3), 914-917. doi: 10.4103/ajns.AJNS_45_18 https://www.ncbi.nlm.nih.gov/pmc/articles/PMC6159074/

27. Northcott, P. A., Robinson, G. W., Kratz, C. P., Mabbott, D. J., Pomeroy, S. L., Clifford, S. C., . . . Pfister, S. M. (2019). Medulloblastoma. *Nature Reviews Disease Primers, 5*(1), 11. doi: 10.1038/s41572-019-0063-6 https://doi.org/10.1038/s41572-019-0063-6

28. *Phoenix, T. N., Patmore, D. M., Boop, S., Boulos, N., Jacus, M. O., Patel, Y. T., . . . Gilbertson, R. J. (2016). Medulloblastoma Genotype Dictates Blood Brain Barrier Phenotype. *Cancer Cell, 29*(4), 508-522. doi: https://doi.org/10.1016/j.ccell.2016.03.002 http://www.sciencedirect.com/science/article/pii/S1535610816300551

29. *Pols, S. Y. C. V., Veelen, M. L. C. v., Aarsen, F. K., Candel, A. G., & Catsman-Berrevoets, C. E. (2017). Risk factors for development of postoperative cerebellar mutism syndrome in children after medulloblastoma surgery. *20*(1), 35. doi: 10.3171/2017.2.peds16605 https://thejns.org/pediatrics/view/journals/j-neurosurg-pediatr/20/1/article-p35.xml

30. Qin, C., Olivencia-Yurvati, A. H., Williams, A. G., Eskildsen, D., Mallet, R. T., & Dasgupta, P. K. (2019). Inline flow sensor for ventriculoperitoneal shunts: Experimental evaluation in swine. *Medical Engineering & Physics, 67*, 66-72. doi: https://doi.org/10.1016/j.medengphy.2019.03.010

31. Riva-Cambrin, J., Detsky, A. S., Lamberti-Pasculli, M., Sargent, M. A., Armstrong, D., Moineddin, R., . . . Drake, J. M. (2009). Predicting postresection hydrocephalus in pediatric patients with posterior fossa tumors. *3*(5), 378. doi: 10.3171/2009.1.peds08298

    https://thejns.org/pediatrics/view/journals/j-neurosurg-pediatr/3/5/article-p378.xml

32. *Schreiber, J. E., Gurney, J. G., Palmer, S. L., Bass, J. K., Wang, M., Chen, S., . . . Gajjar, A. (2014). Examination of risk factors for intellectual and academic outcomes following treatment for pediatric medulloblastoma. *Neuro-Oncology, 16*(8), 1129-1136.

REFERENCE LIST

doi: 10.1093/neuonc/nou006 https://www.ncbi.nlm.nih.gov/pmc/articles/PMC4096173/

33. *Spiteri, M., Guillemaut, J.-Y., Windridge, D., Avula, S., Kumar, R., & Lewis, E. (2019). Fully-Automated Identification of Imaging Biomarkers for Post-Operative Cerebellar Mutism Syndrome Using Longitudinal Paediatric MRI. [journal article]. *Neuroinformatics.* doi: 10.1007/s12021-019-09427-w https://doi.org/10.1007/s12021-019-09427-w

34. *Srinivasan, V. M., Ghali, M. G. Z., North, R. Y., Boghani, Z., Hansen, D., & Lam, S. (2016). Modern management of medulloblastoma: Molecular classification, outcomes, and the role of surgery. *Surgical neurology international, 7*(Suppl 44), S1135-S1141. doi: 10.4103/2152-7806.196922 https://www.ncbi.nlm.nih.gov/pmc/articles/PMC5299153/

35. *Stavinoha, P. L., Askins, M. A., Powell, S. K., Pillay Smiley, N., & Robert, R. S. (2018). Neurocognitive and Psychosocial Outcomes in Pediatric Brain Tumor Survivors. *Bioengineering (Basel, Switzerland), 5*(3), 73. doi: 10.3390/bioengineering5030073 https://www.ncbi.nlm.nih.gov/pmc/articles/PMC6164803/

36. Toescu, S. M., Hales, P. W., Aquilina, K., & Clark, C. A. (2018). Quantitative MRI in post-operative paediatric cerebellar mutism syndrome. *European Journal of Radiology, 108,* 43-51. doi: 10.1016/j.ejrad.2018.09.007 https://doi.org/10.1016/j.ejrad.2018.09.007

37. Whiting, B. A., & Barton, R. A. (2003). The evolution of the cortico-cerebellar complex in primates: anatomical connections predict patterns of correlated evolution. *Journal of Human Evolution, 44*(1), 3-10. doi: https://doi.org/10.1016/S0047-2484(02)00162-8 http://www.sciencedirect.com/science/article/pii/S0047248402001628

38. *Youlden, Danny R. ; Frazier, A. Lindsay ; Gupta, Sumit ; Pritchard-Jones, Kathy ; Kirby, Maria L. ; Baade, Peter D. ; Green,

Adèle C. ; Valery, Patricia C. ; Aitken, Joanne F. Stage at diagnosis for childhood solid cancers in Australia: A population-based study. *Cancer Epidemiology*, April 2019, Vol.59, pp.208-21doi: https://doi.org/10.1016/j.canep.2019.02.013

http://www.sciencedirect.com/science/article/pii/S1877782118305514

About the Author

Trish Carpenter grew up in the south of Brisbane, in Queensland, Australia. A high school teacher of music and history, she lives with her son Cameron, her husband Owen and Penny, their labradoodle. Trish's love of writing brings forth her story which immortalises a young boy's courageous spirit set against the heartbreak of childhood cancer, brain injury, palliative care and grief. Trish is passionate about finding meaning in the journey she has been on with her son Thomas and hopes this story brings some comfort and resonance to other families caring for children with cancer. Her first book, *Big Hand, Little Hand* is for any reader who is looking for insight, inspiration or simply to be moved by a story of love and hope.

www.bighandlittlehand.com.au

www.ingramcontent.com/pod-product-compliance
Lightning Source LLC
Chambersburg PA
CBHW030614110526
44587CB00049B/290